AF413818

THE GOSPEL ACCORDING TO A
SOUTHERN NOBODY

Printed in the United States of America
Keen Vision Publishing, LLC
www.publishwithkvp.com
ISBN: 979-8-9951383-8-9

THE GOSPEL ACCORDING TO A
SOUTHERN NOBODY

LEONARD 'DARIN' BROWN

1
GENESIS: SOUTHERN GRIT

A red dirt winter, cold enough to crack your knuckles just by stepping outside. A one-stoplight town dug into the clay of Sand Mountain, Alabama. Nothing much moved but the wind, and the folks trying to outrun it. Them folks worked themselves to death or drank themselves there. Sometimes, both. If they were lucky, they had a good dog to ride it out with. That was what Sand Mountain, Alabama, had to offer.

Fame stuck to this place like rot on a dying tree. Nothing too special to those who don't know about it, but home to those who knew nothing else. Friday nights under the stadium lights. You could smell the sweat and teenage lies drifting from the concession stand. Folks measured a man by how he hit and if he got back up after. Dances smellin' like cologne and lies. The grocery store was like church. The town was small enough that you knew everyone, or you knew someone who knew their people.

Blood ran shallow. Gossip ran deep. These are my roots.

I came into this world crooked, with one good eye and the other wandering like a drunk uncle at a barbecue, blind and useless. It didn't focus on much. Like it knew early that this world wasn't worth the trouble. Nobody ever figured out what caused it. Folks had opinions. They always do.

They patched my good eye, hoping to guilt the bad one into seeing. Some quack with half a license and a full beard said it'd work. Well, it didn't. I ran into chairs, walls, dogs, people—wore bruises like a second skin. When the patch came off, there wasn't much difference. Turns out you can't scare an eye straight, leaving me with a target painted on my back.

Kids laughed. Adults pitied. I learned early that if you can't be normal, you better be funny. And if you can't be funny, you better be fast. I got quick with my tongue before my legs ever caught up. Not everyone was so appreciative of my gumption.

By third grade, I was catching wood to the backside like it was a sport. Daily. Paddles with names like *The Persuader* and *Old Hickory* met with me often. Got told I was bad. Maybe I was. Or maybe I just saw the world for what it was and couldn't keep my mouth shut about it.

Couldn't explain myself if I tried. Wasn't no diagnosis back then. No ADHD labels or learning plans. Just a look and a swing. If you couldn't sit still, they'd beat the wiggle out of you. School ain't have no patience for none of that mess, and I was made aware early on.

I didn't hate school. I just never fit in. Wasn't a golden boy or a genius. I was the kid turning detention into a roast and the principal's office into a stage. I'd take a swing from a teacher and call it a warm-up. I once taunted a teacher over a paddling, and he took it as a challenge. That was the kind of life I had in school. Took a hit and kept on running my mouth. It was the only way I knew to survive during those years.

Outside school, things were quieter but no softer. Born to quiet parents and a brother eight years older, I had my share of people to look up to.

My old man worked shifts at the plant that'd buckle most backs. Then he'd haul hay for my great-uncle like he owed him penance. He didn't talk much. His hands—cracked, gnarled things that they were—did the talking for him. Always moving. Always building or breaking something.

Mama held the house together as best she could, working hard. She disciplined us when necessary but was always there with a softness that only mothers could carry.

But it was Dad who taught me how to carry weight without complaint. His unspoken words taught me a lot: *"Stand up. Shut up. Keep going."*

He never said much. His silence was a language of its own, one I learned fluently.

We weren't raised soft. We were raised to endure.

And this gospel I'm telling? It ain't clean. Ain't sweet. Ain't strung up in stained glass and hymns. It's mud and spit and blood and busted knuckles. The kind you hear at deer camp or behind the bleachers or whispered over a passed-out buddy in the bed of a truck. It's the gospel of boys who never said, "I'm hurt"—just spat "fuck you" and kept walking.

They named me Leonard Claxton Raye. And if you'll sit a spell, I'll tell you how a blind-eyed Sand Mountain boy made sense of a world that never gave him much more than a seat in the shadows.

2
SNAKE YARDS AND TEASED HAIR

During the years when I couldn't spell my name or tie a bootlace, we lived on a patch of Alabama dirt where snakes outnumbered children and God only visited on Sundays. A singlewide trailer with rusted underpinning and an old screen door that slammed like a pistol shot was what we called home. The carpet clung to smells like it was paid to—smells like fried meat, must, and maybe even fear. That was home sweet home, but it brought much more than most folks could stand.

The land was known. Not for crops or cattle, but copperheads and chicken snakes. Rattlers, if the weather was right. My mama would scan the yard before letting me out like she was prepping for a firefight. Every five minutes, her voice came through the mesh door.

"Watch for snakes! And don't play with 'em! They'll kill you!"

It wasn't a suggestion. I took the warnings to heart, with her words killing any curiosity, I ain't no cat. To this day, a garden hose curled in the grass still makes my skin crawl. The thing about growing up where snakes outnumbered children is you learn quick how to keep your feet moving and your eyes open. Trouble don't always hiss before it bites. Back then, I thought Mama's warning was only about the ones in the yard, but looking back, she was unintentionally warning me to look out for the snakes with smiles instead of scales.

The yard had more than snakes, fortunately.

Out front, there was a rope swing hanging from a limb that looked older than sin. Mama used to sit and swing with me while we waited for my older brother to get home from school. Humming old nursery rhymes, soft like wind through pine. She didn't get many of those days since she had to work. Both my parents did since money wasn't as endless as the snakes surrounding us.

We weren't poor the way city folks imagine, no cardboard signs or soup lines. But it was thin living. No cable, no A/C unless a storm blew cold through the window. First time we got a TV, I was four. Rode in the back of Dad's truck to pick up a tall antenna pole. Burned my legs on the metal and didn't say a word. That was the deal around those parts. Don't whine, don't waste, and hold your end.

It was a way of life that I learned early, even if it didn't always serve me best. I got left with babysitters a lot. First ones weren't kin. It was whoever could be found at the time. Had kids older than me, watching over me, who treated me like something sticky on the bottom of their shoe. I didn't have the words for bullying then. Just knew it felt wrong. But I didn't have to whine 'bout it. The marks they left on my head told the story. Mama saw and pulled me out of there like a lightning bolt in a denim jacket.

That was when my aunt stepped in. Mama's older sister was a holiness woman through and through. She wouldn't wear pants even if it meant outrunning fire. Dresses only. Hair teased up high, sprayed stiff as a trophy. I swear she could knock out a mosquito with that hairdo alone. She prayed like it was a war and loved like it too.

Her husband, my uncle, was all sinew and silence. Outdoorsman. Farmer. Disciple of sweat and Scripture. He believed boys should know the woods before they knew shaving cream. Didn't speak often, but when he did, even the house seemed to listen.

He taught by doing. Long nights catfishing, lines cutting into black water. Lantern glow, frogs chirping, stories whispered like they were sacred texts. He read the river the way other men read bank statements: with reverence.

Rabbit hunts came early. Mornings where the frost still clung to fence posts, dogs whining in the truck bed like sinners wanting grace. He said you had to feel the trail, not just hear it. A real hunt hums in your ribs before it ever hits your ears.

First time my uncle sat me in a clearing and told me to wait for the rabbit, I did. And when it came—soft fur, twitching nose—all I saw was Thumper from *Bambi*. Couldn't pull the trigger.

When he asked if I saw it, I lied. Said I didn't.

He didn't call me out. Just patted my back. "You'll get it when you're ready," he said. And somehow, that stung more than a scolding.

He was full of lessons like that.

One lesson I'll never shake was when he caught my brother and cousin mouthing off to my aunt. She didn't raise her voice.

She prayed instead. But my uncle? He stepped outside, came back with a dog whip. No yelling. No speech. Just said, "Let's go." They followed him out like men to the gallows. Sun was setting behind him like some Southern justice god.

When it was done, they walked in quieter than church mice. Never mouthed off again. That whip didn't just leave marks. It left a memory.

And then there was the frog-leg cookout. I was maybe seven. Didn't know what to expect. My uncle walked into the swamp and came back with a cooler full of croaking. Built a fire beside the barn. Black smoke, snapping limbs.

He fried those legs crispy over the coals. Told stories while the fat hissed and spit. Every part used. Nothing wasted.

We ate under stars, grease on our fingers, and I remember thinking it felt holy. Like communion, if communion came with bones and Coke in a can.

My aunt's church was another thing entirely. Mama dragged me there once. Just once.

It wasn't a service. It was a storm. People shouting, dancing, wailing like they were outrunning demons. The preacher didn't speak—he thundered. Said we were all hell-bound. And the folks there? They didn't run. They danced toward it.

It didn't feel like joy. It felt like panic. I didn't go back. Not for a long time.

Truth is, those early years carved more into me than I could've known. There was love, yeah, but it was flanked by hardship. Crying wasn't encouraged. Work came first. And sometimes, blood didn't mean a damn thing if the love wasn't there to back it.

Mama came from a tribe of hard folks. Seven kids. Not one

made it through school. They didn't drop out. They stepped up. Fields needed hands. Hay needed hauling. Calves needed pulling. They didn't dream about freedom. They learned to live without it.

They weren't bitter. Just busy. And maybe a little mean when they needed to be.

Those were my people.

The lessons didn't come from books. They came from scars and from folks who knew how to swing a dog whip without raising their voice.

3

GHOSTS, GIRLS, AND PADDLE MARKS

We moved into a brick house the year I turned five. Red clay foundation. Rough around the edges. A three-bedroom with enough land to stretch out and make mistakes. Dad said it was a good spot—close enough to the cattle farm for him to work both jobs, far enough out we could piss off the porch if we wanted.

It was the first time we had real space. Not just grass but land. Trees you could climb 'til your arms gave out. Dirt that begged for a shovel. Enough yard to dig your way to China or bury secrets without a soul noticing. I used to believe it was just land. Innocent, empty land. But land in Alabama never comes empty. Not really.

Dad had grown up just over the hill in the old farmhouse. No insulation, just wind and nails holding the place together. He and his brothers used to tear through the woods like they were being chased. Sometimes they were. Not by people. By stories. Shadows. The kind that outlived their tellers.

There was this grave, hidden back in the trees. One old stone, leaning like it was tired of standing. Dad said it belonged to a deserter, some poor bastard caught running from the Civil War. They hanged him right there, on that very land. And when it came time to build our new house, well... they didn't move the grave. Just built on top of it.

No one said that at closing.

I'm not saying I believe in ghosts. But I ain't saying I don't. That house had a hum to it. Like it breathed differently when the sun went down. Air thick enough to chew. The dogs would bark at corners. Lights would blink as if they'd seen something they couldn't explain. The hallway stretched out at night like the spine of some sleeping animal. I kept one eye open. The good one.

Still, that house raised me. Brick by brick. Bruise by bruise. It's where I learned how to swing a hammer. How to keep your mouth shut when Dad was already tired. How to take a hit and not cry. How to give one back when it mattered.

The house held sound like it was saving it for something— mama's gospel in the kitchen, dad's boots in the gravel, the belt drawer sliding open like a shotgun rack. It wasn't a quiet house. Silence never lasted long. Even the ghosts knew to keep it moving.

School started not long after. Only one in town. K through 12, all in one long stretch of government brick. You could walk from kindergarten to high school without ever changing buildings. Just the same smell—Pine-Sol, spoiled milk, and puberty—chasing you down the hall.

There were no clean slates, not in that place. You were who you were, and everybody saw it. They saw you cry the first day. Saw when you peed your pants in first grade. Saw the zit on your chin that took up residency like it paid rent. You don't outgrow your past in a school like that. It just ages with you.

I came in small and mouthy. Good at making people laugh. Bad at shutting up. By third grade, I was a regular at the paddle club. Teachers didn't even pretend to be surprised. Some of them had a name carved into the handle just for me. A few would ask if I wanted to go ahead and get mine early, like a morning stretch.

And I would. Grinning.

"Is that all your weak ass has got?" I said once.

Third grade. Woodshop teacher. Right after, he swung and missed the edge of my pride. I got two more for that one.

Wasn't the star athlete. Wasn't a genius. But I could break a classroom up with a well-timed one-liner. And when you grow up with a crooked eye and a soft heart, that's as close to power as you're gonna get.

We didn't have therapy. We had licks. We didn't have guidance counselors. We had janitors who prayed over us and teachers who kept paddles like heirlooms. It was fall in line or fall flat. I did both, depending on the day.

Looking back, that stretch of school years was about more than just paddles and punchlines. It was where I started learning what hurt really was, just not in the way I expected.

Somewhere around fourth grade, I fell in love for the first time. At least I thought I did.

Susan.

Her name didn't fit her. Sounded soft. Nothing soft about her. Tomboy through and through. Hair tangled. Nails dirty. Fists ready. Could outrun most boys and out-climb the rest. She had a look like she'd seen God and wasn't impressed. And Lord, I was gone.

She never laughed at my jokes. Not once. That might've been why I loved her. I brought her pencils. She told me to give them to someone who actually liked me. There weren't any.

She didn't giggle. Didn't blush. Just rolled her eyes like I was a fly she couldn't quite swat. But I kept chasing her. Even when it made no sense. Especially then. Every time she called me "dummy" or outran me on the field, it hurt a little more, and I loved her a little harder.

That was the first time I started to wonder if I'd ever be enough, not just for her, but for anybody.

Kids laughed when they found out I liked her. Like the idea of a boy like me—tall, one bad eye, soft around the edges—thinking he could win a girl like that was the funniest joke of all.

It stung.

And I laughed with them, like I didn't care.

But I did.

Still do, if I'm being honest.

She never became my girlfriend. Not then. Not ever. But she taught me something: heartbreak don't wait for grown-ups. It shows up early, knocks your knees out, and doesn't say sorry, and sometimes, the people you want most don't look back. Not even once.

At the time, I thought that was the worst kind of pain a boy could feel. But years later, I'd learn different. Losing Susan was just the warm-up. I had no idea heartbreak could cut deeper— or that one day, it would.

That town had its expectations. Every boy wore the name of his father like a badge or a curse. I wasn't the only one trying to measure up. My dad, his brothers, my own brother, they all carried the weight. I was just beginning to feel it. Just starting to understand what it meant.

But that's a story for another time.

One I'd have to face head-on, whether I was ready or not.

4

THE WEIGHT OF THE RAYE NAME

Some names come with pride. Some come with land or money or stories passed down like gospel. Mine came with silence.

The Raye name came with the kind of weight you didn't see 'til your back started to bow. Not all at once. Just slow enough that you never noticed the stoop in your shoulders. Until it was there. Until it had always been there.

On my mother's side, I never met her dad. He passed just a few months before I was born. Her mother died when I was around six. A tough, snuff-dipping, Jesus-loving woman who kept birds as pets. Despite the grit, she was kind. Soft-spoken. The kind of gentle that stuck with you long after she was gone. This side of the family was no less important, but the Raye side of things hit different.

The first time I tasted real loss that stuck with me, I didn't even know what I was chewing. Just knew something was missing. An ache behind the ribs. I was nine when that ache began.

My grandfather and grandmother on my dad's side died close together. The only grandparents I had left. She went first, then him, like the world had to clear her out so he'd know it was time. They'd been split for years, but that didn't seem to matter.

Grandfather was the one I stuck closest to. He made me laugh. Told stories with his feet up and a pipe in his teeth. Braves games on the radio, Crimson Tide on the TV. Marlboro Reds if the pipe was wet. My dad trimmed the old man's toenails when he couldn't reach them anymore. Didn't blink. Just kneeled and did it. That was my dad's way. That was love. Quiet. Not asking for anything in return. Something passed down to him...

Near the end, my grandfather quit smoking. That's how I knew he was dying. Six months later, he was gone. Vietnam and tobacco, hell of a tag team.

Nobody cried. Not out loud. Not where it counted.

I cried. But only when no one was looking. In the car. In the woods. By the headstone. Left notes like I thought the wind might carry 'em somewhere. Sometimes I still imagine he's reading them. Probably laughing at me. Probably lighting another cigarette. From that point on, the ache steadily grew.

One uncle went to prison before my grandfather passed. They let him come to the funeral but only under strict supervision. Shackled and in chains. No one was allowed to approach him. He stood at the edge of it all, like a ghost caught between two lives. I saw him later, behind glass. His voice was softer, like jail scraped the bark off him.

Another uncle left earlier. Cancer. I was seven. I still remember the inside of that truck—diesel, spit cups, old leather that stuck to your legs. He used to let me ride with him on the backroads, like that was all the world there was.

And then the soft one, the great-uncle who owned the cattle farm, worked with Dad at the plant. The one I thought would make it. He felt more like a second father than extended family. We worked with him out on the farm, saw him nearly every day. His presence was constant. Deeply personal. He fell asleep behind the wheel one morning while headed to check out a pair of hunting dogs. Woke up in a hospital bed, paralyzed from the neck down.

Doctors said he'd never make it a year. He made it twenty.

His wife never left his side. That was real love. Not flowers and words, but the kind that changes bedsheets at 2 a.m. and still smiles when you can't smile for yourself.

My cousins, the kids of the uncle in prison, carried the same weight we all did—just heavier somehow. Grew up in the smoke of it. No dad to lean on, mom gone to a brain bleed. They went rough early. Some to drugs. Some to jail. One to a grave before thirty.

The Raye name had its own kind of gravity. And if you weren't careful, it pulled you under.

But through it all, through death, jail, trucks, and wheelchairs, my dad stood different. He didn't talk much. Didn't drink like his brothers. Kept his head down and his family fed. People in town talked about his brothers. But they respected my dad. He wasn't flashy. He showed up. Every day.

I didn't realize it yet, but I was already learning how to carry the weight without folding.

But none of that—not the funerals, not the prison glass, not the bloodlines unraveling—came close to the night I lost my brother, someone I once looked up to, almost like a hero.

It started loud.

My brother came home mean. High on something. His shoulders were tight like he was holding in a storm. He and Mama started up again. They always did. But this time, something cracked open.

My brother grabbed the gun from the cabinet. Got in his truck like he was leaving the world behind. Mama wasn't letting it happen. She opened the passenger door, tried to pull the gun from him. He snapped. Threw the truck in reverse. The door caught Mama like a hammer, slamming her against the tree beside the driveway. I can still hear that sound. Still see her body fold like a paper doll.

And me? I stood there. Frozen.

Not because I didn't care. But because something in me broke before I could move.

She lived. But the brother I knew didn't.

He wasn't dead. Not in the way people talk about. But the boy I'd grown up with, the one I'd hoped might one day be more than just a warning, he was gone. How he went will always stick with me...

Everything had come to a head days before Christmas. Cold outside. A little snow on the ground. My brother came home high or drunk, and this time, he and Dad got into it. I was the one who called 911. I guess I thought I was trying to save someone.

A local city cop showed up, one we all knew. The kind folks called a real-life Barney Fife. My brother tackled him to the floor while I was still holding the wall phone. The dispatcher heard me say, "He just took the cop down," and that's when she sent out the emergency call. Within minutes, the house was swarming with state troopers.

My brother fought them all the way to the squad cars. Didn't make much difference. Arrested him anyhow. He refused bail. And by the time he was released... He wasn't the same.

Different eyes. Different laugh. Like something inside had been scraped clean.

The hardest part of losing someone alive is knowing they're still out there—just not for you.

Another loss that made the weight of the Raye name all the heavier for me...

5

THE CATTLE FARM AND MY DAD'S SILENT STRENGTH

The farm wasn't ours, but we bled enough into the dirt to think otherwise. My great-uncle was left paralyzed, so it fell on my dad to keep the land alive. No court order. No papers signed. Just one man's word and another man's spine giving out.

It started small. Fix a fence here. Move some cows. Run the tractor a few times before a shift. Then it turned into every off-hour, every holiday, every moment when most men would've found a reason not to. My dad never talked much about duty. He just did it. He was the kind of man who measured worth in how much weight he could carry before he buckled—not in dollars, not in praise.

We'd wake up early, me rubbing sleep from my eyes while he was already sipping coffee like it owed him something. He never yelled. Never begged. Just walked past my bedroom door, boots heavy on the floorboards, and that was enough. I'd get up. Pull on the jeans that still smelled like manure from yesterday. Follow him out into the world like it was church.

I didn't get paid. Didn't get thanked, either. I got blistered hands and muscles I didn't ask for. I got looks from other kids who'd never touched a cow but knew every cheat code on Sega. I got tired. But I also got something else, something I wouldn't understand 'til much later.

We had one truck. One dog. About a hundred head of cattle, give or take, and a bull too mean for even my great-uncle to name. The fields stretched out like a quilt someone had stopped sewing halfway through. Ragged at the edges. But they were ours. And I can still smell them on days when the wind shifts just right—hay, mud, diesel fuel, and shit. It ain't romantic, but it's honest.

One winter, I watched a cow trying to push out a calf wrong-way-round. Dad didn't blink. Didn't wait for a vet. Just spit on his hands and shoved his arms so far into that cow I thought he was gonna disappear. Pulled the calf out slick and breathing. Then, like it was nothing, he reached back in and pulled out his watch. Slipped it on like he was checking the time for church. Didn't say a word. Just nodded and walked off to check the fence.

But not all days on the farm came with small victories.

There was one cow, black with a white blaze across her nose, eyes like she knew too much. Smart. Mean. Knew every weak spot in a gate and every slow step in a man. That morning, Dad figured he could handle her himself. He told me to get ready for school and said he'd be back inside before I made it to the driveway.

He wasn't.

By the time I was to step on that school bus, it was clear something was wrong. The house looked still, like the windows were holding their breath. Then I heard Mama. That sound no boy should have to hear from his mother—not anger, not fear, but panic.

Dad had slammed into a metal bar trying to cut that cow off in the chute. Knocked clean out. Blood on the ground. Mud in his mouth. When he came to, he didn't scream or cry. Just stood up, walked to the truck like he'd lost a bet, and drove home.

By the time I saw him, he was at the kitchen table with a towel over his head, the towel more red than white. Mama came over to him and peeled it back, and her face went pale. Said she could see his brain. So, they had to get him fixed. Thirty-six staples, they said later.

That night? He went back to the plant. Clocked in like he always did.

He never talked about it. Never milked it for sympathy. Never even slowed down. It was like he left the pain out there with the cows, buried it in the mud and kept on moving.

And me? I learned something that day. Not from a lesson. Not from a lecture. But from the silence.

Strength wasn't in lifting. It wasn't in yelling. It was in getting up. Even when you shouldn't. Even when your skull's been split open and your body says no.

My dad never raised his voice. But the way he stood? That was loud enough.

6

THE SATURDAY GAME AND MONDAY NIGHT WRASSLIN'

The day that satellite dish landed in our yard, it was like we'd just bought a piece of the future and stuck it in the red dirt. Big gray bastard, all angles and wires, squatting out there like it was hunting signals from Mars. Before that, we had rabbit ears and prayer. A couple of local channels that fuzzed in and out, depending on cloud cover and luck. The picture was never clear, but the yelling from the living room always was.

Back then, Football Saturdays meant packing up and heading down to my great-uncle's place. Lord, he loved the game despite being paralyzed from the neck down and bitter as a snake with a busted fang. Watching football gave him some extra life. Built a room just for it, wide and low, with enough space for a hospital bed and the ghosts he brought with him.

Time spent in bliss. Windows cracked open to let in the fall. Fried chicken grease hung in the air like it belonged there. Sweet tea in sweating glasses. And always—always—Eli Gold's voice spilling from the radio. We didn't watch games the way regular folks did. We muted the TV and let Eli do the talking.

That man's voice was scripture. Dad and my uncle could read a play before the snap like they had the damn playbook in their back pocket. They'd shout before the ball even moved—cuss, praise, spit, and start over.

Sometimes, the preacher came by. Tall, wiry, smelled like peppermints and old Bibles. He'd bless the players, the food, the outcome, and then, two quarters in, he'd turn into a man possessed, cussing out wide receivers and linebackers like they'd insulted his mother and defiled the pulpit. You never heard a man say, "Goddammit, run the damn ball!" with more conviction. It was blasphemy and beauty in the same breath.

And if you mentioned Auburn in that room, you'd better have your affairs in order.

Saturdays were sacred. Didn't matter what else was going on—funerals, weddings, birthdays. You timed it all around kickoff. I once saw a man walk out of his daughter's recital to catch the second quarter. Nobody even blinked.

Christmas meant one thing: Alabama gear. Red caps, gray hoodies, shirts with the elephant snorting fire, and Roll Tide stitched in God's own thread. It was uniform, not a gift. Mandatory. At school during Iron Bowl week, it wasn't "Wear your team shirt." It was "Don't be stupid." Auburn kids stayed quiet or risked blood. If you walked in wearing orange and blue, you might as well have drawn a bullseye on your chest and handed out darts. Some did it just to start something. I admired that from a distance.

It was all part of the code. Family first. Football second. Auburn last.

Then came the dish.

Suddenly, we didn't need my uncle's game room. Didn't

need the trek down the road. We had it all beamed right into our living room like magic. Dad adjusted the thing like he was dialing in the moon. Said it was the best money we'd ever spent. Might've been right.

Those Saturdays watching the game at my uncle's place meant something. They were loud, messy, and full of life. We still saw my great-uncle nearly every day—partly because we worked the farm, partly because he needed the company after his accident. But when that satellite dish came along, something shifted. It brought the game home to us.

Dad, Mama, and me in the same room without the noise of the world pressing in. My brother was around now and then, but by this point, he mostly stayed in his room or was gone altogether. For once, Dad didn't have to go anywhere. He could kick back in his own chair, with his own TV, and still feel like part of the team. Those moments made Saturday special.

But Saturday wasn't the only holy day anymore. Come Monday night, the lights dimmed, and the living room turned into a wrestling ring. We got to enjoy a whole new sport.

Wrasslin'.

Not wrestling.

There's a difference.

Two, maybe three hours of pure, red-blooded chaos. Dad and I watched it like it mattered. Like those matches could solve the world. We flipped between WWF and WCW, arguing over which was better, knowing damn well we'd watch both anyway. He'd grip the arms of that La-Z-Boy like he was in the ring, jaw clenched, body tensed, ready to leap. When Ric Flair strutted out with his big mouth and bigger robes, Dad's laugh would bounce off the walls like a shotgun blast.

And Stone Cold? Lord, have mercy. When that man flipped Vince McMahon the bird, my dad howled so loud the dog pissed himself.

I lived for it.

Not because I believed it was real—though, I did for a while—but because in that moment, I wasn't some kid with a busted eye and a quiet ache behind my ribs. I wasn't the punchline of the schoolyard or the soft target in PE class. I was the one in control. The one in the ring. Sharpshooter locked in. Crowd roaring. My classmate Daniel tapping out like a baby while Susan looked on in wonder.

Yeah. That's what I dreamed.

Wrasslin' gave me that.

Dad would get all wound up during a match, then slump back when it was over and say, "Hell, it's all fake anyway." Like he had to remind himself not to care. But I saw it in his eyes. He did. Maybe more than I did. Maybe that's why he always watched with me. Maybe it wasn't about the match at all.

We didn't have internet yet. No emails. No message boards or YouTube replays. Just satellite and time. And for a boy who wanted out of his own skin, that was enough. Monday night was mine. Sacred in its own way.

And the truth is, I wasn't looking for heroes.

I was looking for a place to breathe.

And for two hours each week, I found it.

7

SAXTON AND THE SUMMER
THAT CHANGED EVERYTHING

I was about eight the first time I met Saxton and his older sister, Kelly. Their grandparents lived just a quarter mile down from our place, land that butted right up against ours. That summer, like many after, Saxton and Kelly were staying there while their parents worked. It was one of those accidental friendships that sticks to your ribs, like fried chicken grease and red clay dust.

We met the way most kids in the country do—on bikes, halfway between his yard and mine. No introductions, no grown-ups. Just the heat of a Southern summer, a dirt road, and a mutual need to burn daylight. Saxton was one year younger and Kelly two years older. Saxton was quick to laugh and quicker to fight, and Kelly had that older sister calm about her, like she'd already seen enough of the world to know how little sense it made.

Saxton would go on to become my best friend, even though we were never in the same class at school. He never made fun of my eye. Somehow, we just clicked. Turns out, our dads and uncles used to run those same woods when they were our age.

Saxton's dad and his brothers knew my dad and my wild-ass uncles from way back—back when they were just a bunch of hell-raising mountain boys themselves.

So, when Saxton and Kelly started spending summers at their grandparents' place, there wasn't much hesitation. His folks knew exactly what kind of trouble my family was capable of... and they didn't say a word. They just let us be. I guess they figured we'd either learn the hard way or come out the other side with stories to tell. Just like they did.

From the first day, it was like we'd always known each other.

One of the biggest moments of our early adventures came the day we discovered the coal mine. We were coyote hunting behind his grandparents' property with our 20-gauge shotguns when we found a path that looked worn but passable, leading about two miles deep into the woods. It was wide enough for a vehicle and overgrown just enough to feel secret. We followed it, hearts pounding with curiosity. At the end of it, we found a massive, long-abandoned coal mine. It had filled with water over the years, forming a deep, oval-shaped pond. One side sloped gradually like a natural boat ramp, while the other ended in a steep cliff.

We stood there speechless, staring at the still water. You could barely see the other end, it was so long. It was quiet. Sacred, almost. We later found out that older kids used to jump off the cliff and swim. That spot would become a cornerstone of our lives. First came the innocent days of fishing and swimming. Then, in the years that followed, it would evolve into something more. The coal mine would play a large part in our teenage years, good and bad.

But back in those early years, it was pure discovery. We felt like explorers. That pond was ours, untouched and unknown. We'd hike out there with PB&J sandwiches and spend the whole day casting lines or daring each other to swim to the far end. It was our hideout from the world, a place where the rules didn't apply.

And as if that wasn't wild enough, one summer, Saxton decided we needed to make our own wine.

Now, understand this: we were around thirteen and as dumb as dirt when it came to alcohol. But Saxton had dial-up internet at his parents' house, a luxury I didn't yet have. He used it to pull up a homemade wine recipe. It may have been written by a lunatic or someone in prison, because the steps made no real sense, but we treated it like gospel. Grape juice, sugar, bread yeast, and some Mason jars from his grandma's pantry. That was it.

We hid the whole setup behind the shed near the barn. Seemed like the perfect hiding place, until it wasn't. His grandpa nearly caught us four different times. Once, Saxton had to fake seeing a snake to stop him from opening the door. Another time, the smell of fermenting grape juice leaked out, and we had to act like we'd spilled something from lunch.

Weeks went by. We checked on our batch like it was a science experiment. Then, one day, Saxton declared it ready.

He handed me the first jar, and I took a sip. It tasted like vinegar mixed with firewood and regret. I'm not exaggerating when I say that single sip might've kick-started my puberty. It burned going down, made my eyes water, and for a minute, I thought I was dying. But I nodded like it was good stuff, because that's what brothers do.

We both gagged and laughed so hard we almost threw up again. That wine was awful, but it was ours. It was freedom in a jar. And it was the first of many little acts of rebellion that would carry us through our teenage years.

That same freedom, ironically, led me to church.

Sometimes, to escape the house on Sundays—and my dad's NASCAR marathon snoring—I'd ride to church with Saxton and his grandparents. At first, it was just an excuse to be with my best friend and avoid listening to engines roar while my dad snoozed like a freight train. But over time, something stuck. That church was my first real experience with faith outside of the summer Bible schools my mama dropped me off at, where the focus was more on Kool-Aid and hot dogs than salvation.

The church felt different from the hardwood of the pews in my aunt's holiness church. It was quieter, slower. That church made me feel *normal*, clean in a way that I hadn't before. Unlike in other places, people at that church didn't laugh when my bad eye drifted in a different direction. For the most part, church folks tried to look past your last name and your appearance, at least sometimes. It made all the Bible talk easier to digest.

I wasn't sure if I believed any of it, but I couldn't deny the pull. Maybe it was the way the Thompsons believed, or maybe it was the hope they carried in the way they sang hymns like they'd never lost anything in their lives. I didn't know what I was looking for, but something about it felt... close.

Eventually, I got saved in that little country church. It didn't stop me from raising hell in the years to come, but it planted something in me. A seed, maybe. One that would grow in its own time. But there's a lot more to tell before we get to redemption. The years to come were miles away from my young head. For now, it was fishing poles, homemade wine, pinecone battles, and the secret world of two boys growing up wild in the hills of northeast Alabama. In those days, it felt like we were invincible. But something was slowly shifting, though I couldn't put my finger on it yet.

Saxton's eyes would sometimes wander off during our late-night talks, like his mind was already a few steps ahead, maybe even beyond the woods we'd spent every day exploring. Things were changing in him and our friendship slowly but surely. A lot of changes were on the horizon, whether I was ready or not.

8

PUBERTY AND PLAYBOY

Middle school didn't walk in quiet. It kicked the damn door down. One day, I was barefoot in the dirt with Saxton, and the next I was waking up to armpit hair, a deepening voice, and dreams I couldn't tell a soul about. Puberty came in loud, like it had a score to settle. My voice cracked like a busted speaker, and I had to have braces *twice.* That's how crooked my teeth were. I looked like a blind pirate with a mouth full of scrap metal.

But worse than the awkward body changes was realizing that my reputation hadn't stayed behind in elementary school—it followed me right into junior high like a shadow I couldn't outrun. The elementary hallways knew me as the class clown with a lazy eye and a mouth that didn't know when to shut up. Now, the junior high hallway was figuring out that same kid had just upgraded schools. And the high school hallway? Well, it was already whispering.

I remember walking through those halls, and it felt different. The air was heavier. Like, even the lockers knew my name. I'd catch little glances, hear the soft smack of whispers behind cupped hands—

"That's the Raye kid."

Not said with awe. More like curiosity. Maybe fear. Maybe pity.

The teachers? They didn't say it, but I saw it in how they paused before calling on me. Like they were bracing for whatever storm I might bring. As for the older kids, high schoolers who had siblings at my school, some of them had already heard the stories—same school, just different hallways, same stories waiting for me around every corner. Stories I hadn't even lived yet. They were just waiting to see if I'd meet the legend or go even further. That reputation wasn't just something I had. It was something everyone expected me to live up to, whether I liked it or not.

It was never just me.

The weight of being a Raye wasn't something you could shake, especially not in a town as small and familiar as ours. It crept up in whispers, in the way folks shifted their eyes when your name came up, in the way teachers seemed to sigh just a little when they saw it on their roll. I'd catch it in my dad's face sometimes—this strange mix of pride and exhaustion. He didn't say much, but I could feel the expectations stacked high, like he was handing me something invisible that he'd been carrying for years.

I didn't think much about it at first. I was too busy being a kid. But once junior high hit, I could feel it pressing down more. It wasn't just about making the team or trying not to screw up in class. It was the way the teachers glanced up when I walked in, like they already had a warning label taped to my back. I started asking myself—am I doing this for me, or am I just trying to make sure the Raye name doesn't sink even lower in the water? That name followed me like a shadow. I tried to outrun it, but most days, it felt like it already knew where I was headed.

The paddlings in seventh and eighth grade weren't like they used to be. They hit harder, carried more behind them. For the first time, I started feeling the consequences in more than just my backside. But I couldn't seem to stop, couldn't seem to shut my mouth and swallow back the snark that rose up. Trouble followed me like a dog that knew I had food in my pocket. And truthfully, some part of me liked it. I liked being known. Even if it was for the wrong reasons.

I started paying more attention to sports, mainly football and basketball. Not just because I liked them, but because of two things: one, most Raye boys had some athletic skill, and I couldn't be the one who didn't. And two, girls. They liked the athletes. And after Daniel stole Susan back in elementary school with just one kiss, I wasn't planning on losing another to someone like him.

I had two female teachers in junior high that we rotated through for certain subjects, and a PE coach who must've thought he was training us for the Olympics. That man ran us like we were prepping for a marathon every single class. But those two women teachers? They were the older, hillbilly, "I'll kick your ass" types. They could've been bodyguards for the Rolling Stones. Most kids feared them when they raised their voices. Me? I was a Raye. Day two of seventh grade, I found myself right back in familiar territory, hallway exile. And just like old times, out came the trusty paddle, holes drilled through it to reduce wind resistance like she was swinging a damn lightsaber.

Let me tell you, that first hit had me squeezing my butt cheeks so tight you'd think I was trying to hold in a hurricane of diarrhea. The sting lit up my spine, but I didn't let it show. That was the Raye in me. If they were going to hit me, I'd give them a show.

Of course, Saxton was still in the picture. Summers hadn't changed that. But this one was different. Voices were changing. And like voices, people had a way of changing. Kelly, his sister, was developing in ways that confused the hell out of us. We were still just boys in a lot of ways—riding bikes, throwing rocks, talking trash—but now there was this undercurrent we didn't understand. Girls didn't feel like just girls anymore. They felt like mysteries wrapped in tight shirts and side glances.

Then came the incident I'd never live down.

One day, I was in their grandparents' house, getting ready to use the restroom, when I heard Kelly's voice from behind a door further down the hallway. I followed her voice. Didn't think much of it, until I pushed the door open, and there she was, standing there with her shirt off, putting on a bra. The world seemed to stop for a second, and my brain scrambled for a way to fix what had just happened. It was my first time seeing a real girl in a bra. And it sure as hell wasn't supposed to be like this.

Kelly screamed and turned red, grabbing for anything to cover herself. I froze, a deer caught in headlights. My mouth opened, but no words came out. This wasn't how I imagined seeing a girl's body, and sure as hell not Kelly's. After that, she wasn't just Saxton's sister anymore. She was... well, something more.

After that day, she went from being "one of the guys" to "damn, I want to date her." But she was older, and I was just her brother's wild, one-eyed, loudmouth friend from the Raye family. Still, it didn't stop me from thinking of what happened or from no longer seeing her as *just* Saxton's older sister.

A few days later, Saxton found out. He approached me, and I knew something was brewing. The look in his eyes was the kind of anger I didn't recognize, even though we'd had our kid fights plenty before. He was mad, but this was different. He punched me in the nose over it. No hesitation, no warning. Just bam.

My head snapped back, and I staggered, the blood knocked out of me. I'd lost that baby fat by this age, and I'd put on more height, so he had to aim higher than usual. But it wasn't the pain that stung the most. It was the realization that he'd just really hit me because I'd somehow crossed a line. He didn't think I was good enough for his sister. And that? That hurt more than the physical hit ever could.

I stood there for a moment, staring at him while blood ran down my face. The Raye in me screamed to fight back, to make him feel it. But for some reason, I didn't. Instead, I just turned around and started walking home. Saxton shouted at me, but the distance between us grew. I didn't go back to his house that summer. I spent the last two weeks in my yard, alone. The silence was comforting. My body was bruised, but more than that, I was still figuring out how to deal with this whole "growing up" thing.

When school started back up, I ran into Saxton again as if nothing had happened. We didn't talk about the punch. It was like we'd both erased it, pretending it hadn't changed anything.

But things weren't done changing. There was the kid, a grade ahead of me, who somehow had a stash of Playboy magazines at his house. I don't know where that kid is now, but I'd put money on him either running a cartel from some Caribbean island or being a tech billionaire no one saw coming. Back then, he was Cool Dude #1. With hormones roaring through me like a freight train, he became my own private dealer. His hustle? Ripping out pages from those magazines and selling them under the table during break and lunch like we were part of some middle school black market.

I had to do more chores than I can count to get a single, crumpled page of some blonde bombshell. But it was worth it. Back then, the internet was dial-up, slow as molasses, and you couldn't just find that stuff like kids can now. I can't tell you how many times I damn near got caught with that page folded up in my back pocket. And Lord, I feel for my mama. I know she had to wash socks from under my bed and just look up to heaven, shaking her head, pretending not to know.

With all that weight riding my shoulders, it made sense that I'd start looking for an escape. Something dumb, something reckless. That was when the stash of crumpled-up magazine pages fell into my lap. It wasn't much, but for a kid like me, it was enough to feel like I was finally in on something. I was beating that thing like it owed me money.

Junior high was confusing and wild, but it was mine. I was surviving it the only way I knew how—laughing through the pain, swinging back when I had to, and learning, piece by piece, what kind of man I might end up being. Even if I wasn't quite ready to face that just yet. Because truth is, that stretch of life wasn't just about hormones or rebellion. It was about identity. Pressure. Figuring out if I could carry the Raye name and still find my own underneath it. Puberty and Playboy were just the backdrop—the noise behind the lesson. The real story was learning how to be more than a reputation, more than a last name. Learning how to look in the mirror and recognize the person staring back once the laughter and chaos finally went quiet.

But the thing about middle school? It doesn't slow down. Before I could even catch my breath, I found myself sliding into something that felt bigger than I was ready for. Something that felt like it would follow me the rest of my life.

9
EXPECTATIONS

Basketball and football were the two things that could make or break you in our town. It was the kind of place where your athletic ability meant just as much as your last name, and for better or worse, I was tangled up in both. I wasn't the biggest kid on the field or the court, but I had enough heart to make people notice, and that mattered—even if it didn't always feel like it.

By the time I hit 8th grade, my athletic side was starting to show. For the first time, sports were helping with the ladies. Back in elementary school, I was an afterthought, more like a background player in everyone else's story. But now I could at least hold a conversation with a few of them. I had finally gotten past the whole "who are you looking at?" phase, where I'd catch someone's eye but my bad eye would drift somewhere else. It felt like I was fighting a battle with my own body just trying to talk to someone.

I wasn't exactly getting dates like the stars of the team, guys like Jacob or Matt, but it was progress. Girls were starting to notice me. Still, I had to wonder, was it really me they were seeing, or just the version of me that showed up on a football field or basketball court? It didn't feel fully real.

I was used to being invisible. Being seen at all felt like a win. Small as it was, it was a step toward belonging. On the court, things started to click.

On Sand Mountain, the air smelled different during football season. It was crisp and full of dirt. The trees and rocks up there had a way of putting everything in perspective. But that didn't stop the weight from pushing down on my chest. The sound of the ball bouncing, the squeak of sneakers, the crack of pads in fall, all of it had rhythm. And I was trying to find mine.

Teammates started taking notice of me, too. I wasn't just the guy riding the bench or getting lit up on option plays. I was starting to prove I belonged.

Jacob, the coach's kid, had it easy. Or it looked that way. Confident, talented, always at the center of attention. Percy, his stepbrother, was constantly trying to match him, trying to outdo him. They had their own spotlight. I wasn't in it. I was just trying to survive drills without screwing up. But being around them raised the bar. The expectation was clear: rise or disappear.

Matt brought something different. He wasn't the top athlete, but he kept the team together. He reminded us to laugh. When things got too serious, Matt was the reset button. That mattered more than people gave him credit for.

Brad had size and power. Everyone expected him to take over varsity when the time came. I didn't need to be Brad. I just didn't want to be forgotten.

Jamie was sharp and smooth. He and I were unofficial enforcers on defense. If someone was getting fouled hard, it was probably one of us. It gave me a role, even if it wasn't glamorous.

Saxton, a year younger, played football like he was trying to kill someone. One summer, he laid me out during a drill. I never saw it coming. That hit stayed with me. It reminded me that expectations didn't always care about age or size. You showed up, or you got run over.

Even with all that, I couldn't shake the feeling that I was still on the outside. The other guys seemed so sure of themselves. I had the ball in my hands, the coach calling my name, but I still felt like a visitor in someone else's world.

That's when I started to get it. Being on the team wasn't just about ability. It was about being present and proving you belonged every single day. Camaraderie wasn't natural. It took time and pain.

One of the biggest tests came during two-a-day practices the summer before 9th grade. The heat was brutal. Those practices were legendary. You either stepped up, or you got left behind. Everyone in town paid attention. It was a proving ground.

That summer, I decided to challenge Adam. He was a senior, all-state, and built like a tank. When the coach called us to line up one-on-one, Adam made a beeline for me. No hesitation.

Sweat poured into my eyes as I crouched down. I had a plan. Hit him hard, knock him back, make a statement. I wanted to show that I belonged.

The whistle blew.

It was over in a second. Adam hit me so hard, I thought my pads weren't even on. I hit the ground, stunned. I couldn't breathe. Couldn't move. I just lay there, watching the clouds spin. Reality check. Adam was 17 and had been dominating since I was in junior high. I was still trying to write my name in the books. But lying there, it wasn't shame I felt. It was clarity. I might never be the biggest, but I could be the one who got back up. Every time.

That was my role. Get hit, get up, go again. In that, I found a kind of peace. Pain meant I was in the game.

But even when things felt tight with the team, pressure never went away. Sports weren't just sports. There were expectations from coaches, from family, from the town. You weren't just playing for yourself. You were playing for how people saw Eagle High. Playing to prove we weren't just hillbillies the Valley kids could laugh at.

The fans didn't help. When we played Valley schools, some of our people would dress up in overalls and boots, leaning into the stereotype like they had something to prove. They yelled things from the stands that weren't just rude. They were ugly.

There was another kind of competition going on. The kind people didn't talk about. It lived in the tension of those games. It showed up in the jokes, in the sneers, in what parents said under their breath.

At the time, Sand Mountain was all white. The Black kids went to schools down in the Valley. We only saw them when we played them in basketball, twice a year. And every time, the hate came out in the open.

Parents shouted racial slurs like it was normal. Some even seemed proud of it. That was the first time I realized the racism we read about in school wasn't history. It was here. It was us.

And it wasn't just the stands.

As I got older, I started seeing the rest of it. The Klan wasn't some ghost story. They were still there, still doing parades, still handing out flyers, still pretending they were just another community group. Sometimes, they were at the four-way stop in robes. Other times, they were selling donuts. People acted like it was just part of the scenery.

My parents didn't say much. When we passed them, the windows stayed up. I think they were trying to protect me, trying not to name it so I wouldn't have to carry it. But I saw it. I felt it. And eventually, I understood it.

Some of the parents of the kids I went to school with wore those robes.

That reality sank in during those games against Valley teams. It wasn't just about sports. It wasn't just a rivalry. It was something deeper, something rotten.

I didn't have the words for it at the time. But I knew it wasn't right. And I knew I'd have to face it again. The Klan and I weren't finished.

But that part comes later.

10

TATER SHED

The summer before my freshman year, I was 15 years old and finally had my learner's permit. On Sand Mountain, that was as good as a full-blown license, especially if you had a job. And lucky me, I did. My parents decided it was time I earned my own money to pay for gas, car insurance, and whatever else I thought I needed. At first, that sounded amazing. Money. My own. But what I didn't understand yet was the harsh world of hourly wages, taxes, gas mileage, and insurance premiums. Took me about a week to realize that the "whatever else" fund I imagined wasn't going to happen.

My job was at the local potato shed, or the "tater shed," as we called it. It wasn't much to look at. Just a big elevated structure that stunk like dirt, sweat, and potatoes baking in the sun. It was about five miles by road from our house, but I could cut through the woods on my four-wheeler and be there in three minutes. Still, I drove the old pickup truck for the sake of coolness. No way was I rolling up on a four-wheeler looking like some backwoods greenhorn. How I passed the driver's eye test to get that permit was a miracle on its own. I remember squinting through the machine. When the lady told me to cover my right eye, I said, "Well, I can't. If I do that, I won't be able to tell you a single letter."

There was a good two minutes of silence behind that counter.

Finally, she shrugged and said, "Well, alright then," and pushed me through.

I mean, you can't deny a Raye his driver's license.

The shed was owned by a local family whose kids went to Eagle High. Paxton was two years older and in Kelly's class. His sister Catherine was in mine. Their parents went to church with Saxton and Kelly's family. Everyone on Sand Mountain knew each other. If you were one of the chosen guys, you got to ride the harvesters—giant, loud machines that looked like monster bugs crawling over the crops. When those boys rolled in at the end of the day, they looked like rockstars, dusty, sweaty, and proud.

I started at the bottom.

That first summer was all about proving myself. Nobody handed you respect at the tater shed—you earned it with sweat, blisters, and a back that ached for days.

The first job was working the trucks that dumped potatoes onto the shed's conveyor. These trucks had V-shaped beds with a small conveyor at the bottom. In theory, the potatoes slid out onto the belt. In reality, they were often muddy and stuck together. You had to pull boards out by hand, dig, stomp, and shove until those taters moved. Two trucks at a time. Quick. Or the field fell behind.

By 10 a.m., I was soaked in sweat. One especially hot day, I was elbow-deep in mud and taters, shirt soaked, deodorant gone, glasses sliding off my nose, when I got that unmistakable gut churn. Something from lunch didn't sit right. I held on as long as I could. Then it was time.

The shed had one bathroom. No A/C. No fan. Just a door, paper-thin toilet paper, and a seat that felt like swamp water. I did what had to be done. Sweating, groaning, praying. Cleanup was its own trauma—wetting that cheap TP like a science experiment.

When I opened the door, there she stood. Rebecca. The most beautiful junior at the shed. She worked the grading station and needed the bathroom right after me. Her face said everything.

And my face? My face said, "Kill me now."

I was a one-eyed, muddy, stinking, defeated soul between her and her next bathroom break. I don't know if she ever looked at me the same. I wouldn't blame her. Didn't stop me from looking, though.

Rebecca was a cheerleader, and so were some of the other girls at the grading station. Their dress code was basically: "Make the boys look." And we did. Hormones were thicker than the humidity. They sat there with music playing, tossing bad taters, laughing, flipping their hair, making sure we noticed every inch. We did. We dreamed about them nightly.

Summer after summer, I worked hard and worked my way up.

By my last summer, I moved up to the palletizer crew. That meant stacking 25-pound bags of potatoes. I thought I was hot stuff. I even started smoking Marlboro Reds like my grandpa. I'd puff one at lunch, lean against the truck, looking like a mini Clint Eastwood. No clue how I survived puffing cigs and slinging bags all day. But it felt cool. Then came the year Paxton's dad landed a huge order for 50-pound bags. Everything sped up. Those bags weren't just heavier. They were alive. Bouncing off the belt like wrecking balls. My biceps, once confident, now begged for mercy. Every day, I went home sore, grumpy, and certain I had permanent back problems.

Paxton always tried to impress his dad. One day, he tried driving the biggest truck on the property, a stick-shift beast he wasn't ready for. He rolled in grinding every gear, spitting dip into a can like he was Dale Earnhardt. Another time, he flattened a gravel patch using the biggest bulldozer his dad owned. Gravel flew. Workers scattered. It was chaos. Even when Paxton's stunts went sideways, a small part of me admired his nerve.

I wasn't innocent either. One time, Saxton and I told Paxton's dad that my dad needed me home urgently. We were already in swim trunks under our jeans. He saw through it but nodded and waved us off. We took off to meet some football buddies at the coal mine cliffs. For a couple of hours, we were free. We weren't just skipping work—we were catching our breath from a world that never slowed down.

Those summers were tough and sweaty. But they taught me more than school ever did. I wasn't cool. I wasn't the star. I was just a nobody with calloused hands and big hopes, clawing to be someone. I wanted to be the guy who ran the shed. The one Paxton's dad couldn't do without. I probably never got there, but I tried.

Each summer taught me something, even if I didn't realize it at the time. By the end, the tater shed felt less like a job and more like a test. It became a place that hammered something steady into me. The tater shed taught me hustle, rank, and how to laugh through the stink. We were just kids playing grown-up in a shed full of potatoes. But it was unforgettable.

53

11

FRESH MEAT AND FIRST IMPRESSIONS

Elementary was all about learning, fighting mentally, and figuring out how to navigate people. Junior high brought a little more advancement—socially, mentally, and in my confidence. But freshman year? That was a whole new jungle. We weren't just kids anymore—we were "fresh meat" for the seniors who ruled the hallways, gyms, and fields like kings and queens. It was survival of the fittest, and I damn sure planned to swim, not sink.

That first morning, I stood in front of the mirror longer than I'd admit, trying to decide if I should play it cool or look like I cared. I told myself I didn't care what people thought, but I was still smoothing my shirt and checking my hair. Freshman year felt like an audition for the next four years, and I didn't want to bomb the opening act. After all, I had spent eight previous years trying to overcome being the kid with one good eye.

Eagle High School was built different. This was the year you switched classes for every subject instead of one teacher running the show. Now, we had lockers, had to find our way through crowded hallways, dodge senior pranks, and somehow remember combinations in between it all. But there was more. Our school pulled in new classmates from surrounding feeder schools. Kids who only went up to 8th grade at their tiny schools and then got shuffled into one of the main high schools around the area.

That meant our tight group—eight years deep together—was about to be diluted. New kids, new talent, new threats. Rumors flew that these new kids were athletes and academic stars. One group even supposedly said they were smarter than us.

I didn't know if they were competition or potential friends, but I knew they were about to change everything. Part of me wanted nothing to do with them. Why mess with a good thing? Another part of me was curious. Would they take our spots on the teams? Would they be cooler than us? I wasn't ready to be second-string in sports or in social standing. I barely had either, and I didn't want to start from scratch all over again, and no Raye had graduated from school yet, and some of my peers knew this.

So yeah, first-day homeroom had tension in the air like a playoff game.

Sitting there, I felt like I was watching a draft—everyone checking each other out, wondering who would end up where in the pecking order. I wasn't scared exactly, but I was on guard. Freshman year was survival, and I didn't plan to get shoved to the bottom of the food chain.

We were given 30 minutes to sit, state our names, and share something about ourselves before being rushed to the gym for the opening assembly. Once in the gym, Principal John took the mic. The man who would end up playing a role in my high school life more than I knew at the time.

He welcomed everyone, then suddenly I heard: "Claxton Raye."

I was mid-googly-eyes at Amanda, the beautiful transfer from Lions Junior High, when it happened. Her reputation preceded her. I was so awestruck and was not prepared for the sudden callout. My name echoed off the gym walls.

"Claxton Raye, where are you?"

I raised my hand, heart pounding. Every eye in the place turned. That's when it hit me. I was wearing a homemade shirt from junior high that read: "Claxton Raye: The Ladies' Man."

Principal John smirked and said, "I hope the antics of elementary and junior high are left there. Right, Claxton?"

I nodded, cheeks red. "Yes, sir."

The room laughed, and the assembly rolled on, but the walk back to homeroom felt different. I had just unintentionally grabbed the spotlight. Maybe that wasn't such a bad thing.

The rest of the day was a blur—finding classes, decoding my locker, getting shoved into a bottom locker at the far end of the hallway (freshmen always got the scraps), and just trying to survive.

I could drive nearly anywhere on Sand Mountain by that point, but the school had rules. You had to be 16 to get a parking spot. The only workaround? Catch a ride with someone else. Luckily, I had an in—Kelly, Saxton's sister, had her license. Saxton was still in 8th grade, riding shotgun, partly because he was her brother, and partly because, well, we all remembered the punch. Not wanting to rock the boat, I took the backseat without complaint. Better than the bus, where seniors made it their mission to torment freshmen. My first semester of classes was mostly normal: Homeroom, English, Science, Math, and Algebra I. The juniors and seniors who played sports had it made. They got "Athletic Training" as their final class of the day. For them, that meant weightlifting, watching films, and drawing up plays. For us underclassmen, that meant catching up after school.

On my first day in Science, I encountered Jamie, one of the new guys from the feeder schools. Sharp-witted, fast with comebacks, and already had the class laughing.

He cracked a line that made even me laugh, and I thought, *'Okay, buddy, slow your roll. That's my turf.'*

Not to be outdone, I waited for the teacher to drop a perfect "that's what she said" setup. I was ready to deliver the line and win the class back.

But just as I opened my mouth, I felt a light tap on my shoulder. A folded note slid under my arm.

Beautiful handwriting, not a guy's. My brain short-circuited.

A girl's note. Was this finally it? I opened it slowly, heart pounding, eyes darting to the signature first: Amanda.

Jackpot!

But as I started reading, the high wore off quickly.

The note read: *"Claxton, as you may know, my father is the pastor at Glory Baptist Church in Rosalie. I would like to invite you to join us this Sunday as we grow our children's program."*

I blinked. Hard.

That was not the love note I imagined. Especially not after I'd been picturing her in her panties earlier that same day.

But hey, it wasn't terrible.

I scribbled a reply: *"That sounds fun."*

As I passed the note back, guilt washed over me. I'd been going to Saxton and Kelly's church off and on. Was I doing this for the wrong reasons?

Then I looked up, saw Amanda's hourglass figure, and decided... yeah, I was doing it for the wrong reasons, and I was okay with that.

Freshman year was underway. And Lord help me, it was already shaping up to be one hell of a ride.

12

FRESHMAN YEAR & THE RETURN OF THE RAYE BLOODLINE

Those first few weeks, our groups stayed the same. We stuck to our original cliques from where we came from. The feeder schools stayed together, and we original Eagles stayed together. Our science teacher thought it would be a good idea to separate us for labs and classwork, which helped to shake things up a bit, and after a few weeks, you'd have never known the difference. We all fell in line with minimum head-butting.

As usual, I was quick to make fun of myself to break the ice and save myself from embarrassment. But Jamie, he was quick to notice something I had never really thought about.

I had no earlobes. Yeah, I never knew that was a thing to be noticed, but apparently, it was. Jamie honed in like a bloodhound that scented insecurities. Another defect added to the list... But as always, I tried not to let my upset show. Had other things to keep my mind busy.

Our learned intelligence of navigating around the juniors and seniors also improved, except during after-school practice and in the field house. I felt less pressure on the sports side since I wasn't expected to be anything more than a bench warmer on the varsity teams, as the upperclassmen had all the starting positions. But in the back of my mind, I knew this was only temporary.

The field house pranks, though, were notorious and unavoidable. One afternoon, I returned to the field house after practice to take off my equipment and change into my street clothes. But when I went to grab my stuff, I realized my clothes were nowhere to be found. Where did they go? Oh, that's right, they were on top of my dad's truck, which was parked across the two-lane main road that cut through town. So, there I was, in my undies, tank top, and socks, waiting for the cars to go by as I waited at the crosswalk to get to my truck and my clothes. Talk about a shitshow. It wasn't just me, though.

No one was safe from the pranks. Matt got got, too. We were all taking a muscle-gain supplement called creatine in hopes of putting on some muscle mass. But little did Matt know, his jug of creatine had been replaced with baby formula powder. That went on for two weeks, and Matt earned the nickname "Big Baby." He wasn't too happy about it, but it was all in good fun.

The "Plug," on the other hand, was the only one not messed with. Even as a freshman, he was incredibly strong, stocky, and a headhunter on the field. He didn't take shit from anyone, and as a result, the upperclassmen left him alone.

Part of me was starting to enjoy the lack of expectations mixed with harmless fun, but little did I know this would only last so long. Somehow, I even got elected Freshman Class President. It sounds cool, but honestly, we didn't do much. We had two meetings, and the senior class president basically just told us what to do during those meetings.

It wasn't until later in my freshman year that the Raye bloodline showed up with a vengeance.

It started off as just a normal day. I rode in with Saxton and Kelly, made it through the first two blocks of classes, and then, while I was in line with my lunch tray, something happened that changed everything. A sophomore named Paul knocked my tray to the floor in front of everyone and laughed with his friends, making some snide comment about my uncle, who was serving life in prison.

Let me set the scene: this mountain town is small; everyone knows everyone, and Paul just so happened to be the nephew of the man my uncle had shot and killed. So yeah, he and I were never going to be friends, even though I had nothing to do with it. All through lunch, I was seething; in the past, I would've laughed it off or made a joke, but something was different this time.

I wasn't sure why, but anger had taken over; my stomach was tight, my hands were hot, and a voice in my head—maybe mama's—was telling me to walk away, be a bigger person; another voice, louder, sounded like dad on a bad day, carried the weight every Raye ever had, something to prove, said, "Handle it."

I was Freshman Class President; two-sport athlete; riding with a junior girl to school; Amanda liked me (or so I thought); and mostly important, a FUCKING Raye. There was no way I could let the disrespect go unchecked.

After school, I found Paul and beelined straight for him. I grabbed the back of his hair and spun him around. Years of watching WWE flooded back to me. I hit him in the stomach, placed his head between my legs, wrapped my arms around his stomach, picked him up, and power-bombed him, slamming him back-first onto a teacher's table outside the building. Kids were stunned. Some ran, some cheered, and some laughed. Principal John picked me up by the back of my pants and carried me, handbag in hand, to the office.

My parents were called. I received four paddlings and was sentenced to one week at the alternative school in the Valley, where they send the bad eggs from all the county schools.

Paul didn't mess with me anymore, but my streak of goodness came crashing down.

Sitting in that office with my ears still ringing, I didn't feel victorious. I felt... settled, maybe. Like I'd evened the score, but also like I'd just painted a target on my back. Part of me was proud for standing up for myself—hell, for my family name— but another part knew I'd handed Principal John and every teacher in that building a reason to watch me closer. If I had the chance to do it again? I'd like to say I'd walk away. But at fifteen, being a Raye meant handling it. And I handled it.

13

THE PULPIT AND THE POWERBOMB

Outside of school during my freshman year, I started attending Sunday services at Glory Baptist Church. At first, it was just a way to keep tabs on Amanda—she went every week, and I figured if I was gonna chase, I might as well follow the trail to the Lord's house. But the moment I stepped inside, something hit me different. The service felt alive in a way my old church never did. The music had heat, the preacher had passion, and the congregation had soul. It wasn't just hymns and hush. There was movement in the room, like the air itself was shifting with something bigger than us.

Now, Amanda didn't dress quite the same for church as she did for school, but even in modest skirts and that damn angelic smile, she was a knockout. Every teenage hormone in my body stood up and saluted when she walked in. I thought I was making progress—thought we had a connection growing from school to the sanctuary. But what I didn't realize was that I wasn't the only one circling the flame.

Percy, who had always been the golden boy. The athlete, the big shot, the junior high MVP who had always tried to one-up his stepbrother Jacob. He was after her too. And he wasn't just looking to flirt. He was aiming higher. He was gunning for the preacher's daughter like it was the ultimate prize.

While I was busy misreading Amanda's friendliness as flirtation, Percy was planting real roots. She laughed at his jokes, leaned in when he talked. Looking back now, it was clear as day. I was a side story in her week, a well-meaning benchwarmer while Percy played varsity in her heart.

But here's the twist: somewhere between the gospel songs and side-eye glances, something stirred in me. It wasn't Amanda. It wasn't even Percy. It was the feeling that maybe, just maybe, I was being called to preach. I'd heard scripture all my life, had it drilled into me like multiplication tables, but that day, it sounded new. It sounded like a message wrapped just for me.

So, I did it. I stood up in front of that congregation—with Amanda's dad staring me down and the Glory Baptist crowd holding their breath—and I said it out loud. I wanted to preach. I wanted to carry the Word. You could've heard a pin drop. And then, just like that, the place erupted in cheers. Hugs, handshakes, hallelujahs. It felt like the whole town had my back.

Except... they didn't.

What I didn't know was that behind those smiles were whispers. The same folks who clapped the loudest were the first to roll their eyes when my back was turned. I was a Raye. A rough one. Too dirty, too immature, too messed up to be claiming the pulpit. Some said it outright. Others let it leak through sideways comments and cold shoulders. Even the ones who once paid me to speak at community churches started to fade away, like maybe they realized they'd backed the wrong horse.

Amanda? She had opinions, too. And after I power-bombed Paul through a table at school, that was the final straw. Any chance I had with her—any shred of preacher credibility I was clinging to—went up in flames.

Amanda didn't come right out and call me a thug or tell me I'd embarrassed her, but she didn't have to. The looks, whispers, avoidance not just by her but everyone was deafening. I convinced myself that I had made it past the Raye image, the bad eye, the no earlobes and the general how I "look" but I didn't. It was an illusion and I came crashing back to earth and treated like a sinner outcast in some biblical verse.

That one moment, that one table, was all the church needed to burn me alive in the court of holy opinion.

It stung, not just because of what they said, but because I believed in what I was doing. I studied the Bible, listened to sermons, and poured myself into the Word. It wasn't a joke to me. It wasn't just a phase. Maybe I misread the calling. Hell, I misread a lot of things that year—but my heart was in it.

And then came the punishment. It wasn't just one kind. It came from two angles. First, there was the school punishment. A week's sentence at the alternative school down in the Valley. Thirty-five minutes every morning just to walk into that brick-walled halfway house for the misfits, the screwups, and the forgotten. It felt like exile. Like I was being tossed out of the real world and into a place where the forgotten gathered, where you couldn't escape the label.

But that wasn't the only punishment I faced. The so-called Christians turned their backs on me, too. The whispers followed me everywhere. Some didn't say it outright, but I could feel it. I could see it in the eyes of the people who once called me their own. The church that had felt like home suddenly felt like a prison of its own.

At first, I kept going, hoping the whispers would die down. I'd show up, shake hands, try to look unbothered. But the longer I stayed, the more I realized I wasn't part of the family anymore. The warmth was gone. People who once pulled me into conversations now nodded from a distance. Invites started to "disappear," and my sins somehow mattered more than theirs. Not long after that, I started finding excuses not to go—late nights, homework, anything to avoid that feeling of walking into a room where I was no longer welcome.

In the middle of both kinds of punishment, I felt like I was being buried alive—exiled by the people who once had my back. It was a crushing weight, and I didn't know if I could carry it.

But in that desert, just when I thought I had no one left on my side, I found someone unexpected—someone who didn't fit into the neat little boxes everyone else lived in. Someone who saw *me* and not my last mistake.

14

SILENCE AND CONNECTION

That first day dragged like a funeral. Nothing to read, nothing to look at but the moldy drywall and my own damn thoughts—mainly about the 15 stupid-ass minutes that landed me here. Bet the good ol' God-fearing folks back at Glory Baptist would've loved to see me now. As if being stuck in that place wasn't punishment enough, I had to sit there, in silence, with nothing but the smell of old locker room gymnasium and the heavy scent of bleach mixed with something less pleasant, like boiled hot dog water. The walls were so cracked and moldy, they looked like they'd given up trying to be anything more than a holding pen for kids like me.

The room was full of other kids, kids who looked just as out of place as me. We were all here for some reason or another— misfits, screwups, and the forgotten. The kind of kids who didn't quite fit into Eagle High School or any of the other schools in the county. A retired military guy, probably one step away from being a drill sergeant, was in charge. No smiles, no conversation, just a routine. Every day felt like it would never end.

Lunch came on a foam tray—one vegetable, usually something bland like green beans, an apple, and some mystery meat. A slice of school pizza, or a plain hamburger, or two chicken fingers that looked like they came from a factory, not a farm. If you were still hungry, too bad. No snacks, no sodas. You could just wait until you got home.

I was in a cubicle that had been used by two of my cousins before me. The third Raye to sit in that spot. The place was straight-up depressing—like an old, rundown movie set for a jailhouse flick. There were buckets placed in corners to catch the leaks when it rained, and bats would fly through the rafters in search of a place to sleep.

I wasn't prepared for any of this. I didn't know to bring a book, so that first day dragged on forever. I spent the hours staring at the old, moldy walls around me, trying not to go crazy. You could hear the occasional turn of a page or a kid coughing. Sometimes, if someone made too much noise, the instructor would come over, bark at them to be quiet, and then leave just as fast. We all just kept our heads down, did our time, and prayed we'd get back to school soon enough.

On that first day, I couldn't help but replay over and over how the hell I ended up in this mess. What had I done in those 15 minutes that had sent me here? Those 15 minutes had cost me so much. The real punishment wasn't just being in this hellhole. It was the shame of knowing the Christians from Glory Baptist, the ones who had once told me they'd be praying for me, would probably get some sick satisfaction from seeing me now.

Then, something unexpected happened. I met someone I never imagined.

Aaliyah.

Her voice broke through the silence. It was the sound of a female voice asking for a bathroom break.

I glanced to my right to see her standing up, gliding past my cubicle with an effortless grace. My head almost twisted off as I watched her—she had the looks of Jada Pinkett Smith from *Set It Off.* She had a way about her that made you feel like you were being seen in a way no one else had ever seen you before. I couldn't help it. I kept staring, even though I tried not to. I was still scared my lazy eye might give me away.

When she came back from the bathroom, she spun around, cutting through the sea of kids like she was on a mission. She looked right at me.

"So, Mountain Boy... you're from the mountain, right? What's your name?"

I froze, not knowing how to respond. I'd taken too long, I guess, because before I could speak, Aaliyah hit me with another question.

"Well, do you talk? Which high school are you from?"

I stammered out my name and where I was from. She fired off questions like she was interrogating me, walking toward a car that was waiting for her. We kept answering, back and forth, her questions coming faster than I could keep up, until she stopped in front of her car.

Before I could say anything else, she just looked me in the eye, smirking.

"I hope you look at me tomorrow the way you did earlier today," she said, getting into the car and driving away before I could even process what had just happened.

After that first day, I was hooked. I looked for any excuse to bump into her again. I'd time my restroom breaks, hoping we'd cross paths. I'll show up early to just chat with her. We'd linger outside after our day was done, just so she could "educate" me on music. I had some burned CDs Saxton had made for me—mostly rock and pop—and Aaliyah would laugh at my choice of songs, telling me all about the music I was missing. She introduced me to *106 & Park* on BET, because all I knew about was *TRL* on MTV.

By the third day, I was already falling into the rhythm of seeing her. The rest of the days flew by. We'd sneak in extra conversations, her teaching me what it meant to appreciate music, her laughter ringing in my ears long after she was gone. It felt like we were the only two people in that damn building who cared about anything outside the walls.

Aaliyah never asked about my insecurities. She didn't care about the things that haunted me. Instead, we talked about why we were there. Her reason was simple—she'd been tardy too many times, and the principal, some power-hungry white guy, had finally had enough and handed her five days at this place. Even if our reasons for being there weren't good, mine more than hers, I was glad it happened, glad I met her.

Her presence didn't just help me with the church fallout. No, it reached deeper, into my life as a whole. It was the first time I felt that pull, that rush of butterflies, for someone of a different ethnicity than my own. The way she interacted with me, the way she spoke, was unlike anyone I had ever known.

Back at my school, some kids bragged about their so-called "Klan card"—a physical membership card given to them by a Klan member to boost their numbers—something I never understood. What I saw in her, and heard from her, was a soul a hundred times more beautiful than most of those bragging kids back home. She gave me something I didn't think possible at that time. She gave me acceptance without hesitation or question, and I needed it more than ever.

But on day five, everything changed. Aaliyah told me her dad was coming home from the army soon, and she'd be leaving to live with him. The thought of it hit me hard. We never got to explore the possibility of what could've been. The quiet, secret thoughts I had about showing her my home and the high school were just that—thoughts. Because deep down, I knew the mountain was a place that held its secrets close, and she'd be disrespected, whispered about, and unsafe.

We didn't have cell phones then, so I gave her my home telephone number. But after day five, I never saw her again. She did call once or so I was told, but before my mama could ask who she was or for a callback, she had already hung up.

In those five days, though, Aaliyah taught me more about life and myself than most of my friends or even my family ever could.

When she left, it was like someone had cut the lights in a room I didn't even realize had been lit. Five days isn't long, but it was enough to make me hope she'd walk back through that door. Part of me felt like I'd been through a breakup I didn't have the right to claim. No promises made, no real romance, just the kind of connection you don't get often and don't forget easily. Even now, I sometimes wonder what might've happened if her dad's orders had been different.

15

THE RAYE HUSTLE

Summer before sophomore year, I was 16, had my driver's license, and rolled around in a used Isuzu Rodeo SUV my dad found for a steal. I used to complain about gas prices—back when 95 cents a gallon felt high. Hell, if only I'd known.

It was the summertime, and while I had a bunch of people I could hit up or see around town, there were really just four I hung out with regularly: Saxton, of course; Percy (who wouldn't shut up about Amanda, his new girl, and it always felt like a jab); Jacob (who was working his way through girls from our school and two counties over like he had a checklist); and Ryan.

We'd all known each other for years in one way or another—sports teams, classes, or just being from the same small mountain community—but it was during freshman year that we really became a unit. Saxton and I were already inseparable. Percy was tied to us through Jacob, and Jacob had a knack for bringing people into the fold, whether they belonged there or not. Ryan slid in later, through football practice, and stuck because he had a way of making every day feel like an adventure. Ryan was different. He played sports, too, but he didn't let it define him. His family wasn't local—they were from the Louisiana bayou. Unlike the rest of the mountain boys bumping Hank Jr. or Red Hot Chili Peppers, Ryan had me riding shotgun listening to Master P and the whole No Limit crew. Where Aaliyah had opened the door to Tupac and Biggie, Ryan baptized me in Cash Money and controversy. We'd ride around blasting Eminem while others maxed out their stock stereos playing "A Country Boy Can Survive."

These were my boys. When summer came along, it wasn't a question of who I was hanging out with. It was understood that if one of us was doing something, the rest of us were either there or on the way, and that summer, I stumbled across something that would change all of us.

Sand Mountain was a dry area, which meant if you wanted alcohol, you had two choices: drive 35 minutes down either side of the mountain to the nearest town that sold it, or take your chances with the bootlegger, and hope you didn't get shortchanged or busted.

By then, I'd been smoking cigarettes for about a year. And that's where the hustle idea sparked. I realized I was rarely carded anymore. I looked older than 16... maybe not 21, but hell, it was worth testing. We always heard about the field parties the upperclassmen had—rare, legendary things—and it was always because getting alcohol up the mountain was a pain. But what if I could be the one to solve that?

Saxton and I had built this little cabin near the coal mine (not the swimming hole cliffside). We had four makeshift beds, a heat source, real walls, a strong roof, a front door, and even a porch. It was our fort, our haven, our clubhouse. In those early months, we'd just camp out and dream about the day we'd get invited to one of those big-deal parties. But what if, instead, we threw the party?

So, one afternoon, with the Raye blood heating up in my chest, I drove down the mountain. Across the Tennessee River. Right up to the liquor store sitting just outside the city in the Valley.

I pulled into the parking lot slow, real slow. Guess I thought that's how grown folks bought beer. Sat in the SUV for ten minutes, running through every worst-case scenario I could think of:

What if my dad drove by?

What if a family member saw me?

What if my brother was in there?

What if they carded me and called the cops?

What if I didn't have enough money?

What the hell kind of beer do people even drink?

Then, in true Raye fashion, I said to myself, "Screw it. Go get the party started."

The next part was something I wish I'd never done.

I took off my glasses.

Thought I'd look older without them, but I forgot just how blind I was. I mean, legally blind. I had to damn near press my nose to the cooler doors just to read the labels. I was squinting, sweating, damn near hyperventilating.

And it hit me. I never asked what kind of beer I should even get. Looking into those coolers felt like trying to read ancient scrolls underwater. Some cases were red, some blue, some fancy, some cheap. Twelve-packs, six-packs, tall boys—I had no clue what I was looking at. Just fuzzy blobs with price tags.

After what felt like twenty minutes, I spotted something that said "Lemonade." I thought, *'Hey, who doesn't like lemonade?'* It looked like six bottles, seemed easy to carry, and sounded like something people might like. So, I grabbed two.

I made my way to the counter, trying to look calm and grown. Meanwhile, I was sweating like I'd just run a marathon in July. The guy at the register was older, probably had seen every hustle there was. He rang it up and told me the price. I fumbled through my wallet and came up $2 short. Panic mode activated.

"Oh—sorry!" I said, reaching into my pocket and thankfully pulling out a crumpled $5 bill. "Here, just keep the change."

He took it, nodded, and then, just as I reached for the bags, he looked up and said, "So, you like these?"

Stunned. Deer in headlights.

I decided a dash of honesty might help.

"First time trying 'em," I said. "So... I'll let you know."

And then I stumbled out the door.

SUCCESS!

I kept my composure, walking back to my SUV, and slid my glasses back on. I kept my head down and pulled back toward the main highway that would carry me back toward the mountain. I couldn't help but feel triumphant, as if finding my footing, my purpose. I felt seen, like I had something unique that no one else could offer. It was exhilarating, and I knew it wouldn't be my last run.

With the goods secured, it was time to meet up and celebrate the success of the mission.

It was a Friday night, and with only 12 bottles, common sense told us this couldn't feed a full-blown mountain party, so we kept it small with the usual players—Saxton, Ryan, Percy, Plug, and Jacob.

Each of us told our folks we were camping again. With that taken care of, we all made our way through the woods and down the trail until we reached the coal mine. Saxton gathered the wood and built the fire like he always did. Percy cleaned the old tin pots and prepped the canned meals we'd heat up over the flames. Jacob, true to his nature, brought out a couple of reels and tossed a line or two into the dark water, hoping we might snag a catfish or bream to throw over the fire. And Ryan and I? We were in charge of "prepping the beer."

As I scrounged around the cabin for something—*anything*—to get the caps off the bottles, Ryan lit up a cigarette, looked at me with that sly Cajun grin of his, and without saying a word, twisted the cap clean off the one in his hand. He passed it to me like a torch, grabbed another, and did the same. That moment felt weirdly ceremonial, like we were walking into something new and dangerous but exciting all the same.

Once we all had our drinks, we clinked bottles like they were made of gold and took a deep breath. Then we turned them up.

Nobody warns you about that first real taste of alcohol. Not the ads, not the older guys, and definitely not your dad's half-finished can you snuck a sip from on a long ride when you were seven. That lemonade label lied like hell. It wasn't sweet. It wasn't refreshing. It was sharp and bitter, and it hit my throat like a match being struck. My mouth puckered like I'd bitten into a green persimmon, and the warmth sliding down my chest made my stomach flip. But I wasn't about to be the one to make a face or spit it out.

I took a deep drag off my cigarette, nodded, and said, "Hell yeah, that'll hit the spot."

Ryan just chuckled and said, "Told you, man. No Limit Soldier style."

Twelve bottles didn't last long between six teenage boys, but it was enough to light us up. That lightheaded, giggly, loose feeling took over and made everything feel better, dumber, funnier. We laughed about school, about Coach's tight shorts, about what girls wore that drove us crazy, and who had done what with who, which, of course, turned into a competition of lies. Jacob was halfway to being a full-blown adult in his stories. According to him, he'd been with girls from all over our county and had apparently taught them all something new.

We played music from a beat-up speaker I kept in the cabin—Blink-182, Big Tymers, a little Eminem, and even some Manson when it got late. Plug tried to freestyle, and we all roasted him, but secretly, we thought it wasn't half bad. The fire cracked. The stars burned bright overhead. And for those few hours, we didn't worry about anything but that moment.

Eventually, we drifted off to sleep—some in the makeshift beds, others just on the porch or near the fire, using rolled-up hoodies as pillows.

The next morning hit different.

We all woke up groggy, reeking of smoke, and feeling like our heads were stuffed with cotton. Those twelve beer bottles were scattered around like trophies from a war. That was when the paranoia set in.

"What if somebody finds 'em?" Jacob asked.

"What if they test the dirt and find beer juice?" Plug said, only half-joking.

So, in true overthinking teenage fashion, we dug a shallow grave and buried the bottles like we were hiding a crime. Six teenage boys digging in the woods to hide twelve beers. We even marked the spot with a broken tree limb in case we ever needed to check on them again.

We made our way back home, one by one, bloodshot-eyed and quiet, and by mid-afternoon, we were already planning the next one.

The Coal Mine Blowout.

That was what we called it. Next time, it wouldn't just be us. Next time, we'd invite people—girls, upperclassmen, if we could manage it. Maybe even try to get Jacob's cousin to bring a boombox that actually had some bass. Saxton said he'd bring more food. Percy swore he'd bring a girl. Plug said he was gonna freestyle battle anyone who came. And me? I was the supplier now.

The man with the connection.

The guy who'd figured it out.

The Claxton Raye.

We had a place. We had a crew. Now, all we needed was a party worth remembering.

16
THE SOUND OF SOPHOMORE YEAR

Sophomore year had kicked off, and with some saved-up cash, Saxton's dial-up Google skills, and a whole lot of questioning at that electronics shop down in the Valley, Ryan and I finally felt confident enough to make the move. We were gonna build a system. Not just any system—the system. Two Rockford Fosgate 12-inch woofers, a top-of-the-line 500-watt amp, bridged for max amperage to hit both speakers, and a custom box we'd build ourselves to mount it all up in the back of my Isuzu Rodeo.

The goal was simple: Make damn sure you heard me coming down the road, and maybe start a little side hustle while we were at it.

We set up shop behind the house. Borrowed tools from my dad's shed, snuck a few cigs behind the tool bench (because I still believed—somehow—that my parents didn't know), and got to work. It was about three hours of trial and error, yelling, cussing, asking, "You sure that wire goes there?", and arguing over diagrams we barely understood. But when the sun started dipping and that last wire got screwed down tight, we stepped back and admired our Frankenstein. We believed we finished it. Then came the real test.

We cranked the Rodeo, picked a CD. It had to be the right one, preferably something my mama wouldn't give me another 30-minute mind-rotting lecture over. She knew more about Eminem than we did and wasn't shy about calling him out during dinner, usually somewhere between mashed potatoes and "what kind of boy are you turning into?" It was a routine I became familiar with.

But nothing was going to stop us from realizing our dream. Ryan, grinning like a kid with a secret, pulled out his Bass Test CD—nothing but raw, deep, speaker-shattering instrumentals.

"Let's see what this does," he said, slotting the disc in.

We'd even installed a kill switch—tucked right beside my seat—because the Valley had a noise ordinance that'd hand you a ticket just for having your subwoofer humming at a red light. That switch let us shut it down when we saw blue lights.

CD in. Switch flipped.

At first, it was clean, louder than anything we'd ever heard in person, but still controlled. And then the bass dropped.

My dad, in the house a full 10 yards away, peeked his head out the back door, looking absolutely lost. His mouth was moving, but we couldn't hear a single word. Mid-sentence, the bass hit again—BOOOOOOMMMMM—and I watched his mouth say something that looked a lot like, "You're gonna fuck up your damn..." but who knows. We were in it.

I looked in the rearview mirror, and the damn thing was shaking so hard the reflection looked like a mirage in summer heat. Ryan and I locked eyes from the front seats, and I swear to God, the wind off that speaker blast moved our hair like we were in a wind tunnel.

It was perfect.

And we knew exactly how to make our big debut.

We waited until the following school day, a sunny Monday morning in September. No clouds. Calm air. The kind of day where the smallest noise carried. I planned it out like a military operation, timing everything down to the second.

Traffic always clogged the little two-lane road into Eagle High right before first bell, but then it'd clear up like clockwork. I stopped by the usual gas station where I bought my Marlboro Reds and filled up, but this time, I wasn't in a rush. I even walked a lap around the store, grabbed a cold bottle of Coke, and another hard pack of coolness. It was go time. I had a statement to make.

For me, music spoke when I couldn't, or when I didn't want to. It said things better than I ever could. If "Raye" was what they expected, then Raye was exactly what I would give them— loud, raw, and unapologetic, with dirty, provocative lyrics to match. I was a No Limit Soldier fighting to be something.

First bell rang. Road cleared.

I checked the time on my Pioneer CD player, selected the track, Jay-Z and UGK's "Big Pimpin,'" then rolled up slow. I was about 100 yards out from campus. Paused the song. Flipped the switch. Unpaused.

The bass hit exactly where it was supposed to.

School windows shook. Classrooms full of students from 7th to 12th grade pressed to the glass to see what the hell was coming. Teachers peeked out of doors like there was a damn earthquake. I turned into the school lot like I was leading a parade float through town. The **BOOM BOOM BOOM** echoed off every brick wall of Eagle High.

Before I even reached my sophomore parking spot, Principal John and two teachers were already outside waiting for me. Their eyes drilled through the windshield. They weren't mad. Not yet. They were in awe... and trying real hard not to show it.

I cut the amp. Stepped out smooth. Took a long drag off my Red, blew the smoke straight up into the blue Alabama sky, and flicked the butt across the pavement like I was lighting up a movie scene. Walked straight toward them like I didn't have a care in the world.

Another layer of the Raye legend fulfilled.

Within two days, a new school-wide rule was printed and sent home: "All vehicle sound systems must be turned down to minimal levels upon entering school property to preserve the educational environment."

But that didn't stop Ryan and me. Nope.

Within a week, we had our first client. Then a second. Word spread that if you wanted bass in your ride, you didn't go to a shop. You came to us.

And just like that, the Raye & Ryan Custom Audio Garage (unofficial name, of course) was born.

17

THE PRESSURE COOKER

Midway through sophomore year, things started to buckle. Life and school became a pressure cooker.

The more popular I got, the more eyes were on me, and not just the good kind. Popularity didn't cancel out insecurity. If anything, it made it worse. People expected me to be "on" all the time. Funny. Confident. Cool. But underneath, I was slipping—especially in sports. I was falling behind in drills, getting outplayed by teammates, and starting to dread practice more than look forward to it.

Then came the kicker: I needed a job.

Since I was little—four or five maybe—I'd watched my dad work himself to the bone. Swing shifts. Every bit of overtime he could snatch. He worked at Norandal Aluminum, the biggest employer in the Valley, part of the Steel Workers union like most everyone else there. I never knew exactly what he did behind those gates, but the grit on his face and the soot on his uniform when he came home told me it wasn't easy work.

It was dangerous, too. My great-uncle—before his crash accident—had molten aluminum poured into his work boot once. Had to be airlifted out to save his leg. It wasn't some cushy factory gig. This was heavy metal, high heat, and hard labor. Every few years, the union and management would clash, strikes would roll out, and somehow—eventually—it all got worked out without anyone losing too much.

But sophomore year, that changed.

One night, right before the third shift crew was supposed to clock in, the gates at Norandal were locked. Security guards stood inside the fence this time. My dad was part of the crowd of about 200 workers who gathered, confused and angry, outside the plant. Within an hour, the union leadership was notified— the Steel Workers were no longer needed. Negotiations? Terminated. Just like that.

No warning. No final paycheck. No compromise.

Because of how it was done, the company didn't owe full hourly wages either. The union tried to cover employees with its own funds based on seniority, but that wasn't gonna last forever. Still, at first, nobody panicked. This sort of thing had happened before... it always got resolved eventually.

But this time was different.

News crews from Huntsville and Chattanooga pulled into the Valley. They set up shop outside the plant as protest lines formed. Dad and I were there. We held those signs. We booed and shouted at the trucks that kept rolling in, delivering raw material to a place we'd once called our bread and butter. We were there one dusky afternoon when someone—still don't know who—launched a rocket through the fence and into the Cadillac of one of Norandal's management team.

That car exploded into a fireball that lit up the whole sky. I'll never forget that sound. That glow.

sure if I'd ever speak it fluently again. In the Raye family—my brother, uncles, cousins—sports had always been part of the story. Basketball, baseball, football... nobody was a "star," but they all played, started, and made memories that still got told at family gatherings. I had just hung all of that up, and on the mountain, sports were everything.

Nowadays, I still look back and I'm proud of my time playing. I trained myself to play basketball and football, all while learning how to adapt with one blind eye and a weak one to back that one up. If you're ever curious how tough that might've been, next time you're outside shooting hoops or tossing a football, try it with one eye closed and the other one squinted for more than twenty minutes. Let me know how you do.

So, with sports officially off the agenda and my afternoons tied up until 9 or 10 p.m. most nights, I narrowed it down to two things: First, I was gonna be the first Raye to graduate high school...

And second, me and my friends were gonna have a blast before that day came.

18

THE PARTY PLAN

After that first successful beer run, the wheels were officially in motion. Between Blockbuster shifts and after-school schemes, we pulled off six or seven more runs over the next few weeks. Each time, we stepped it up. More beer, better brands when we could afford it. Natural Light, Busch, Budweiser when we were feeling rich. And the invite list? That grew too.

But I already knew from previous experience that beer alone wouldn't cut it. Not if we wanted a party that lasted, a party people would never forget. So, a new plan was hatched.

Kelly's class was about to graduate. Somebody, somewhere, was guaranteed to throw at least one party out in some random field. There'd be a bonfire. Music. Someone's dad's work truck with the tailgate down and the speakers up. But it'd only last until those familiar blue lights pierced through the tree line, and then it'd be over. Like clockwork, people would scatter like roaches to light. The party would be over like that.

I couldn't let that happen to our party.

Ours had to be different. The spot we had at the coal mine

was perfect. We had the parking lot about two miles from the cabin. We had four-wheel-drive trucks and ATVs to transport people to and from the party spot. Not to mention, we'd run enough trial versions to know the flow blindfolded.

However, multiple cases of beer and nothing else wouldn't sustain a crowd once things really kicked off. Liquor was a *must*.

So, that week, I planned to make two separate runs—each trip loaded with four bottles of liquor and four cases of beer. I had a plan: I would play it cool while the old man at the counter, who always rang me up, checked out my purchases. I'd act like I was stocking up for a buddy's birthday bash. I'd even ask him what bottle he recommended and go with whatever he said. All that kept looping in my head: *Keep it casual. Keep it moving.*

While we prepped for the party, I still had other things to focus on. So, while Saxton, Ryan, Plug, and the crew debated logistics—who'd park where, who'd keep an eye on the trailhead, who was in charge of music—I was living a second life down in the Valley. Life at Blockbuster.

We had five hourly workers, two shift managers, one co-manager, and one store manager. I was the baby of my work group at 17. The store sat in a strip center next to Wal-Mart, Goody's, a shoe store, and a handful of food joints, such as Papa John's, Krystal, and Arby's. We'd call Papa John's at least twice a month to complain about botched pizza orders, trying to score free pies. Eventually, it became such a running joke that we started trading early access to unreleased rental movies for food.

I was one of three guys who worked there. Both the co-manager and store manager, Trish and Jackie, were older, married women who loved cigarettes... and "other stuff." They ran the place with a strange mix of apathy and power, but they never gave me too hard a time. Our shift managers were Brad and Sue. Brad was cool. Sue had a mustache and gave off principal vibes, but she was harmless.

Then there was the hourly crew: me, Rob, Shaley, Chloe, and Ava. All Valley kids. I was the only one from the mountain, and they made sure I knew it. My nickname? Mountain Boy.

Chloe and Ava cornered me in my first week on shift, lowkey trying to figure out if I was the "hood in the closet" type. You know, whether I had a white sheet with eye holes hanging back home. Once they figured out I wasn't, we all became tight. Like, really tight.

Eventually, we started hanging out outside of work. And let's just say... corporate Blockbuster would've freaked if they knew what went on. We got into things. Whether it was slipping unreleased movies to friends, starting lowkey bidding wars for the last copy of a new release, or what happened behind that backroom curtain—those nights got wild.

And you learned a lot about people by what they rented. Sometimes, they'd come up to the counter confident. Other times, they'd avoid eye contact, clearly embarrassed by whatever late-night fantasy they were feeding. You could tell who was honest, who was lonely, and who was just horny by a stack of VHS cases.

But my real education came after work.

Brent, Rob, Chloe, and Shaley liked to hit the Mexican joint down the strip for drinks. The owner let me tag along even though I was underage—our little "free rentals for margaritas" deal kept everyone happy. That's where I graduated from Natty Light and Busch to tequila, vodka, gin, and whiskey. I didn't know brands yet, but I knew how those margaritas hit, how vodka and OJ made laughs last longer, how whiskey made secrets easier to share.

The whole time, I kept thinking back to the mountain and how to use what I learned for the parties.

If beer was the bait, liquor was the hook. This was how we'd keep people there long after the music started. How we'd make sure the coal mine party wasn't just another bonfire busted up by blue lights.

And maybe, just maybe, it was how I'd prove I wasn't just 'Mountain Boy with one eye,' but someone who could balance being both the 'good' and the 'bad' Raye.

19

AWKWARD DISCOVERIES

Around this time, I'd made some bases on the field of sex, but the homerun had not yet been achieved. I was in the box once, and the pitcher lobbed one, slow and straight—but I'd forgotten the bat, if you know what I mean. After that night, protection stayed in my wallet at all times.

For me, it wasn't as easy as the likes of Jacob, Ryan, and the others. They loved telling their stories. My stories? They fell way short in comparison. Sure, I had advanced past using the satellite at home to find that half-scrambled channel just to catch a blurry boob or hear a few seconds of moaning, but I hadn't yet been fully intimate in real life.

I thought the coal mine party would be the moment to finally change how girls saw me. But before that night ever arrived, I got sidetracked by something much more personal—a first experience that left me fumbling with nerves, gratitude, and a brand-new insecurity I hadn't bargained for.

Two weeks before the end of my sophomore year—exactly fifteen days before our first large party at the coal mine—Ava and I decided to catch a movie one random night. I got cut early from the store, she was off and bored, and this wasn't anything new for us. Any or all of us Blockbuster crew hung out pretty regularly, so this felt like another night. I was cool as a cucumber, not for one second imagining something could happen.

Ava was stick-built, small butt and boobs, and a different hairstyle every week. Tattooed. Belly-button pierced. Ran track in high school. She was in junior college nearby. Dark-skinned. Green eyes. Real unique look.

We hit the theater on a low-key, non-weekend night. Minimum foot traffic, except for the occasional theater worker. We were seeing *Love and Basketball*—a movie I later found out she'd already seen twice during its first week. There were maybe six people in the whole place. She picked an aisle way further back than we usually sat.

She passed on popcorn until about twenty minutes in, then started reaching over for my small buttery bag. She wasn't talking much—which was weird—but I figured she really liked the movie. I gotta admit, it was good. I was into it.

Looking back now, I realize I was missing every single sign she was giving me to take charge. Then she moved the armrest between our seats and slid over just enough for her leg and arm to press against mine.

What I thought was her hand reaching for popcorn turned out to be a hand on my you-know-what. I was so startled that I dropped the popcorn. She laughed as I fumbled around, caught somewhere between shock and awe, not sure what to say or do.

This was Ava—the older girl from work, in college (even if it was junior college), while I was just the skinny dork from a mountain high school. But I pulled it together, leaned toward her, and... Well, let's just say it wasn't a homerun. But it was the first time I experienced what the adults of my time referred to as "receiving a Southern kiss."

After the movie, things were awkward for a few seconds, right up until we got back in her car. Then she laughed and playfully asked, "You okay, Mountain Boy?"

Trying to play it cool, I replied, "Of course. Thank you."

Then my mind screamed, *'Did you just say THANK YOU for a BJ?!'* Smoke might as well have exploded from my ears.

She just laughed again and said, "Thank you, huh? First time, sounds like."

Boy... what would those old backwoods mountain brethren think about this?

She laughed and blushed, joking, "They're gonna kick you off the mountain."

Then she reminded me to stay cool and not let this be a weird thing.

Did she really know me? Of course, I was going to make this weird.

And just when I thought my nerves were calming down, she hit me with the bombshell that shook any remaining confidence I had left:

"You know, yours is... different than others."

She went into detail, but this book isn't a part of that *Fifty Shades of Grey* lifestyle. But her words set off a storm of thoughts. I'd never looked at another guy's junk. Porn back then was mostly scrambled or came in the form of stolen Playboy magazines. So, how was I supposed to know?

The next 12 hours were filled with deep investigation. Family encyclopedias. Embarrassing half-questions to the guys. Hints dropped to my dad. Eventually, I pieced it together: It was called hypospadias.

Yep. Suddenly, not only did I have one eye that drifts, attached earlobes, and no longer played sports—but now I had *this*, too. Fantastic.

20

THE NIGHT OF THE PARTY

The days leading up to the party kicked off phase one of the plan: get the alcohol. The word had already started spreading through Eagle High about another cabin party. We'd laid the groundwork, hinted just enough to stir curiosity without saying too much. That was the trick: buzz without blame. But that meant no room for failure. I had backup plans stashed away that no one from Eagle High knew about, which involved my Blockbuster team. A couple of them were of age and could buy booze legally. So, why didn't I just ask them?

Two reasons: One, I liked the thrill. *Clearly.* And two, I was determined to keep those two worlds apart. If my high school friends found out about my Valley crew, they'd want to tag along. And if my Blockbuster friends knew what kind of parties we threw, they'd laugh us off the planet. They wouldn't get why we got half-drunk off cheap beer and drove thirty minutes into nowhere for a good time. And honestly, I didn't want them to.

I walked into the liquor store like always—no glasses. By

that point, I'd memorized the blurry labels I needed and what they should cost. But as I reached the counter, my stomach sank.

He wasn't here.

My mind immediately screamed, *'Oh shit. Busted.'*

I tried to play it cool, asking casually, "Where's the old man today?"

The new guy, maybe mid-40s, looked up from the register. "You mean James? He's got a doctor's appointment today. Took the day off. Don't think I've seen you in here before."

"Yeah, never seen you either," I replied. My voice cracked a little. "Ol' James and I are tight. You must work the daytime shift or somethin'."

He laughed. "Yeah, I pull the day shift. James could make friends with a skunk." Then he looked at the stack in my arms. "That's a lotta cases. Someone havin' a party?"

"Funny you ask," I said quickly. "We're throwing a surprise birthday thing for a friend. Just tryin' to get it ready ahead of time."

He nodded. "You need liquor, too?"

I nodded. "Yeah... uh, what do you recommend?"

"What does your friend like?"

Thinking fast, I said, "We're makin' a mix for everybody. Like a punch."

He grinned. "Oh, hunch punch, huh? Clear Springs 190'll do the trick."

Didn't know what the hell that was, but I nodded and told him, "Yeah, that'll work. Gimme four."

He blinked. "Four? That punch's gonna be lethal. You tryin' to drop panties or put folks in a coma?"

I forced a chuckle. "If we don't use it, I'll save it for next time."

I walked out of that store with four cases of beer and four pints of something I'd later find out was 190-proof grain alcohol.

Later in the week, I made my second stop. James was back behind the register. I kept it simple this time—just asked for cheap vodka. No questions. In and out.

Then came the last day of sophomore year. Graduation for the seniors was held that afternoon on the football field. Afterward, three big parties were planned around town. Ours was one of them. The other two were well-known, thrown by established party crews. But ours... ours had buzz.

I checked myself out of school early—learned that loophole earlier in the year. I was home alone, stressing. The weight of what could go wrong pressed on my chest like a boulder. I rehearsed lies. I mapped backup plans. Then the phone rang.

Our house phone. Corded. Landline.

My heart skipped. I thought maybe it was one of the boys calling to go over the final plan.

"Is this Claxton?" a voice said.

It wasn't one of the boys. The voice continued.

"This is Trish. Can you work tonight?"

I froze. Never in all my time at Blockbuster had Trish asked me to work. I just showed up when I was scheduled and asked off when I needed to. And that night, I had asked off.

"Ava is sick and can't come in," Trish added, reading the silence.

My mind raced. I wondered, *'What would my dad do?'* And instantly knew the answer. He'd go. Every time. That man never said no to work. Hell, Brent—the manager on duty—would have to close by himself on a Friday night without me.

I swallowed. "Yeah. I'll be there."

Hung up the phone. My heart sank.

So, I had to drive 45 minutes into the Valley with eight cases of beer and eight bottles of liquor, stash them, and get back before dark. If they weren't on ice before sundown, we risked everything.

I called Saxton. No answer.

Could try his RAZR flip phone, but that'd cost him minutes, and his mom would kill him. Nights and weekends weren't free yet.

I slipped into my Blockbuster polo, left a note on the kitchen counter: *"Went to work, camping with Saxton after."* Then I made the call I had to make.

Saxton picked up. "Make it quick. This better be good."

I blurted out, "Got to work. Stuff by the old chicken shed on dirt road. Under blue tarp. See you when I get off." And I hung up.

Work was packed. Valley kids flooded in since the Mountain schools had graduation. Brent and I were getting slammed. Every second dragged.

All I could think about was the party. The setup. The alcohol. The risk.

Finally, closing time. Brent tallied the drawers and asked if I wanted to join him, Rob, and Shaley for margaritas.

I made up something about a family thing in the morning and bounced.

Crossed the Tennessee River bridge, took the turn up the mountain, and finally—finally—sped up. The curves, the darkness, the deer—I didn't care. I knew these roads like the back of my hand. No cops, no worries.

But just as I crested the final hill, I saw it.

Fire.

Not just any fire. A shape. A symbol.

A cross.

The moment I saw that fire in the shape of a cross, the gut-wrenching mix of confusion, anger, and fear hit me all at once. For a few minutes, the party was forgotten.

I killed the music. My headlights flickered across the edge of a field. The glow stretched into the night. Figures moved in the distance—cloaked in shadow, too far to make out clearly.

My throat tightened. I hadn't seen that sight since I was a kid. I remembered being a kid, maybe seven or eight, riding in the backseat of my parents' car, ducking down as we drove through the four-way stop near my home. Those hoods terrified me even then.

It had been years since I'd really heard the name "KKK," outside of vague comments, offhand remarks, or quiet, ugly jokes. People joked about the Klan still being up here, but deep down, everyone knew. An aunt, a teacher, a drunk, a pastor, a mayor—somebody still had that robe in their closet. Nobody talked about it, not loudly anyway.

This night was different, though. This was no whisper. This was the first time in a long time I saw it manifest in front of me—a rally, a meeting, or whatever they called their gathering.

It wasn't normal. But it wasn't shocking either. That was the most damning part. And tonight, for whatever reason, they'd decided to show themselves.

The blaze lit up the dark night, eerie and unshakable, and in its glow, I could see the white hoods moving almost in unison in the distance. My stomach twisted. I wanted to slow down, stare longer, maybe even make sense of it—but what sense was there to make? I knew what it was. I knew who they were. And I also knew I couldn't do a damn thing about it.

So, I did the only thing I could. I tightened my grip on the wheel and tried to shove it down. Tried to think of the things I had planned. *'Focus on the party. Focus on the music, the cars, the girls. Tonight has to be different. Don't let their hate ruin the night.'* Tried to focus on anything but what I had just seen.

By the time I turned off onto the dirt road toward the cabin, I'd convinced myself that nothing was wrong, as best as I could anyway. I was back in mission mode, ready to make the night a good one.

The road dipped into the hollow, and my headlights swept across the field where we usually parked.

My jaw dropped.

Cars. Everywhere.

I couldn't count them all.

I knew the drill. My SUV was the sound system for the party—had to be near the cabin. My spot. My role.

As I crept past the rows of vehicles, one car stopped me cold.

Amanda's.

The pastor's daughter. The girl who once looked down on me because of my last name, who hadn't spoken a real word to me since the squabble with Paul.

Back then, her silence stung worse than the rumors. It was one thing for the guys to run their mouths—it was another when Amanda, who I once thought might actually see me, suddenly treated me like I was invisible.

And now? There she was, parked and ready to party, same as everyone else.

I shook my head, a bitter laugh caught in my throat. *'Guess the rules only apply until the music starts.'*

Part of me wanted to roll right past and never give her a second glance. Another part—the part that still remembered what it felt like to be dismissed—burned to prove something. Maybe to her, maybe to myself.

Either way, I didn't have the luxury to figure it out right then, not with cars filling the field, not with the weight of the night pressing in.

Time to flip the switch. Time to party.

21

THE AFTERMATH

The flip of the amp switch dropped the beat just as I pulled up toward the center of the party. It felt like the moment a rockstar lead singer hits the stage—cheers, flashes, anticipation. As I tossed the SUV into park and opened the driver-side door, the echo of the bass bounced off the silent coal mine water like we had concert-grade speakers set up out there.

I stepped out, peeled off my Blockbuster polo, and tossed it in the backseat. I started digging for the old camouflage cutoff I'd thrown in earlier for just this kind of wardrobe change. As my eyes scanned the crowd, checking to see who was there and if folks were vibing, I noticed a few girls—ones who came solo—side-eyeing me with quiet little grins while I stood shirtless mid-change. I smiled to myself. This was going to be a good night.

Ryan was the first to greet me, holding up a can of Dr. Thunder like it was some trophy. I looked at him sideways.

"Cheap soda? Where's the beer?"

Without saying a word, Ryan tilted the aluminum can

toward my mouth, signaling me to take a sip. I was thirsty, so why not? But the moment that fizzy liquid hit my tongue, my chest ignited. I staggered back, coughing and gripping my stomach.

"What the fuck?" I whispered, eyes watering.

Ryan gave a wide grin, telling me, "Clear Springs 190. Party starter. Go slow. This shit is STRONG."

No kidding. That first hit alone blurred the edges of reality. Still burning inside, I found Saxton and Plug inside the cabin, managing the booze with precision. This time, they remembered the ice. Coolers were stocked, people were grinning, and some held cans of Dr. Thunder or Mountain Lightning just like mine. But now I knew what was really inside them.

Plug had his vodka distribution system down—eye-measured shots into Solo cups for the ladies, mixed with soda and ice. Saxton had taken charge of the 190-proof, making sure only the main contributors or paying guys got access. That stuff floated right on top of the soda, so the first two or three sips were like straight-up shots. We didn't yet grasp just how strong this stuff was.

We had a bonfire roaring, people dancing, couples sneaking off into the woods, groups singing along to whatever song blasted next—rock, rap, R&B—you name it. The laughter was thick in the air, from freshmen to just-graduated seniors. And us, the hosts? We were royalty.

The 4-wheelers kept buzzing in and out, shuttling partygoers down to the cabin. At one point, it felt like half of Eagle High was there. I walked back to my SUV to check on the music source and make sure the battery wasn't dying. That was when the smell hit me.

It was overpowering—like the time our dog got sprayed by a skunk, but times ten. I panicked, thinking maybe a whole family of skunks had invaded. But then I saw them. Kids standing in a circle near my SUV, smoke curling in the air, passing something around, coughing and laughing.

"Claxton! Jump in the rotation!" Matt shouted over the music.

I hesitated. I'd never touched drugs. Not once. My brother, my uncle—that path ruined them. It was the last part of the Raye curse I hadn't fallen into. But the night had gone so right. Everyone was happy. Nobody had to know.

So, I crushed my cigarette, stepped into the circle, and took the joint when it reached me. No instruction manual, no warning label. Just me, a circle of friends, and the bassline of "Bling Bling" rattling the night air. I inhaled deep—probably too deep.

By my second pass, I knew I needed to sit down. Everything was shifting around me, beneath me, engulfing me.

Underneath the haze, my chest twisted with a different kind of burn. My mind dimly recalled how I had always sworn I wouldn't go down the same path as my brother and uncle. How touching or using any type of drug was the last Raye line I hadn't crossed. But there I was—high, spinning, and pretending it didn't matter. Part of me felt sick about it. Another part felt like I'd finally blended in with everyone else. I didn't know if that was victory or defeat.

That left-handed smoke, combined with the Clear Springs cocktail, shot me straight into orbit. My thoughts spiraled and time warped. One moment it was 10:30 p.m., then suddenly midnight... then 1 a.m., and there stood Amanda and Jacob.

Jacob—our old friend, too busy for us with sports, and Amanda—the pastor's daughter, the girl whose family hated my name. But there she was, drink in hand, grinding on Jacob to "Back That Azz Up" like she'd never heard of Sunday morning.

I stumbled their way, and they lit up like I was Juvenile himself. But I just tossed whatever was left in my drink in their direction, walked past without a word, and didn't look back. It felt good. Real good.

They were gone soon after.

The rest of the night unraveled in flashes—faces blurring, music pounding, lights from four-wheelers cutting through the trees. Then nothing. Just blank space.

Next thing I knew, I was facedown in the dirt, three feet from the cabin porch...

My head throbbed, my stomach churned, and I was sticky with sweat. I heard a few voices, low and slow, and realized the crowd was gone. All that remained were the stragglers—empty Solo cups floating in the water, trash scattered everywhere.

I pushed myself up and wiped the dirt off my face and glasses, and Ryan showed up, wrapping his arm around my neck.

"We did it," he said, proud. "Pumped till about 3 am. Last four-wheeler left at 3:30."

I checked my watch: 9 a.m. Saturday.

Panic.

If my dad came looking, we'd be dead. I pulled the remaining seven of us together, surveying the wreckage around the cabin—beer cans, cigarette butts, trampled grass, a stray wallet, even a lost purse.

Saxton and I knew we couldn't leave it like this. No way.

His parents would bulldoze the cabin if they found it like this.

Then Plug shouted, "I got trash bags!"

We all grabbed three each. We picked up what we could, tossed forgotten belongings in the back of my SUV, and Matt said he'd handle the evidence.

Only... he didn't.

Turns out, trusting the stoner of the group to get rid of evidence wasn't the best call. Those bags? He tossed them into my uncle's cattle pasture two miles down the road.

Guess who found them the next day?

My brother.

Dead to me, but still very much alive and ready to blow the whole thing wide open.

22
RAZOR-THIN LINE

I hadn't spoken but a handful of sentences to my brother since the incident with my mother and his time in jail. He'd been around, but never in my mind or part of my life. As I've said before, he had died to me years ago—but apparently that didn't stop him from being a pain in my ass once I hit my teenage years. My brother, older by eight years, clearly has some deep-rooted issues about the way he grew up compared to me.

In his world, I was the golden child, the favorite, while he was the castaway. But that version of the story was one he wrote himself through the choices he made. I didn't owe him a damn thing. Where he followed the same crooked current many of the Raye men before us had taken, I was swimming upstream, doing things differently. I dropped sports—something nobody in our family had done—I held down a job, which he never managed, and I was on track to be the first Raye with a high school diploma. Hell, the word "college" was even starting to circle through the house.

Sure, I had my run-ins with teachers and school officials,

but I hadn't assaulted a cop. I wasn't feared because of my fists or known for sports domination, but I still had my own version of popularity—built on reputation and my ability to host the best damn parties in town. I had also earned trust in other areas, like with older folks and city officials around the Valley. But putting trust in our friendly stoner friend Matt turned out to be a mistake, one that was about to take some clever navigating to fix.

I came home that morning about the same time those garbage bags full of last night's wreckage were tossed out of Matt's car. Looking back, I'm sure my dad had to know something was up. Mama? She was clueless. But Dad? He just quietly pointed me toward the bathroom and nudged me along.

I looked like hell—bloodshot eyes, reeking of beer and smoke, caked in dirt and God knows what. My stomach churned, my head pounded, and I probably smelled like I'd been sleeping in a ditch—which, honestly, wasn't far from the truth. I took what had to be the longest shower of my life, and as the hot water started to turn cold, I finally dragged myself out. I needed an excuse to get out of the house and nap somewhere else so Mama wouldn't see the zombie I had become. But I didn't need to—Dad took her for a Sunday drive in the box Chevy to go visit family.

Alone at last, I crashed in my bed and started replaying the chaos from the night before. Just as I drifted off, I heard someone swing the back door open—hard. Then came the rustling of plastic bags, followed by a voice I rarely heard but never wanted to: "Hey Claxton, what do you think Mom and Dad would say about these?"

I shot out of bed like I'd been electrocuted. The sight of

my brother standing in the kitchen with those bags in hand made me want to keep sprinting and dropkick him through the damn wall. But he was older, stronger, and, more importantly, holding the smoking gun from last night.

He knew. And he knew what those bags could do. One phone call, one guilt trip to Mama, and it was game over—grounded until graduation. So, I had to go diplomatic.

"Where's Dad?" he asked.

"They went to visit family," I answered dryly.

"Oh, so you're just here nursing your little hangover like a rockstar, huh?"

"Look... just tell me what you want and give me those bags."

"Nah," he said. "That'd be too easy. You ain't got nothing I want."

But I knew better. He always wanted something. And my word meant something to our parents, which gave me leverage.

"What do you need this time—money? A car?"

He paused, that smug grin creeping onto his face. "You convince them to get me a mobile home. Set it up somewhere so I can move out, and I'll trash the bags."

A mobile home?! I couldn't believe what I was hearing. But he had me. In those bags was the remainder of my freedom. If I said no, it was over. Work and home. No more in between. So, I said yes. I laid it on thick to my parents about how my brother was trying, how he needed a second chance.

A few months later, he had his single-wide, and I got the bags back for disposal like they were cursed relics. That summer, heading into my junior year, we kept the parties smaller, but they were still just as wild. I spent more time off the mountain than on it, becoming a shift manager at Blockbuster and spending more time with older friends than high school ones.

Brent and I got tight that summer. Nearly every day, we would go out to hit restaurants and bars in the Valley. We kept bumping into city officials and politicians. I was 17, sipping whiskey with the Chief of Police and City Council members, lifting my pinky on a dirty martini. This mountain kid was living a whole different life.

Slacks and ties over soft jazz at dinner, then cutoffs and tank tops at the cabin parties blasting "Hard to Handle" and "Sippin' on Some Syrup". I was living a double life, and loving it.

Then came the climax of that summer: the city gala. I hadn't even known such an event existed months earlier, but I had an invite. Brent did too. It was held at the city rec center overlooking the Tennessee River. This was suit-and-tie territory. I trimmed my beard, combed my hair, slapped on some cologne and deodorant, and tried to look halfway respectable.

No questions were asked when we arrived. We were seated near the front with the fire chief, city manager, and other top brass. I was by far the youngest person there. Even the barkeeps were older. But there I was, a 17-year-old with a whiskey sour in hand, pretending to follow talk about fire department budgets.

Some folks thought they recognized me.

"Aren't you a manager at Walmart?" they'd ask.

I'd nod and run with whatever version made them comfortable. Brent and I soaked up every drop of top-shelf liquor and gourmet food—though I couldn't understand why rich people gave you such tiny portions.

Then, just when I thought the night was winding down, an auction started. They were auctioning off unopened bottles of alcohol from the event, parading three bottles across the stage.

Someone yelled, "$100!" and it was on.

I looked at Brent. We were both more drunk than we should've been. I told him, "I'm winning this. But we gotta store it at your place."

He laughed, and I started bidding.

$125, $150, $175... I kept going until $285 finally sealed the deal. Everyone clapped. I had just spent what felt like a small fortune—with no cash in my pocket. I prayed they'd accept a starter check and wouldn't cash it immediately.

Brent and I smoothed things over, dropped the check, and left as quickly as possible. I was a minor who had just won a liquor auction at a city event. Back at Brent's place, we opened the boxes: over forty bottles of premium booze. Gin, vodka, bourbon, tequila—no bottom shelf in sight.

We toasted a couple of bottles—nothing crazy, just enough to taste our winnings—but I knew I couldn't hang around long. My parents thought I was at work, and I'd already pushed it later than I should've. I loaded into my car, checked my breath in the mirror, and pulled out of Brent's driveway with a stomach full of nerves and liquor.

The first twenty minutes were a blur of streetlights and slow jazz still ringing in my head from the gala. But the deeper into the country I drove, the darker the road got. Streetlights vanished. Civilization melted behind me.

It was just me and the night.

I cracked the window, letting in the cool air, hoping it would sober me up enough to feel in control. It didn't. My head still buzzed. My eyes felt heavy. My hands, gripping the steering wheel, were a little too tight, with knuckles pale in the dim glow of the dashboard.

That's when it happened.

I was flicking ash from a Marlboro out the window when the cigarette slipped, tumbled in like it had a death wish, and disappeared under my seat.

"Shit—" I muttered, patting the floor with one hand while steering with the other.

I couldn't just leave it. The smell alone would rat me out the second I walked through the door. So, I pulled over on the shoulder, hazards blinking red against the trees, and leaned down to dig it out.

And then I saw them.

Blue lights.

I froze mid-reach, my heart thudding in my chest so loud it felt like it might echo through the trees. I sat up slowly, real slow, like the car was full of landmines.

In my mirror, a cruiser had crept up behind me—silent, no siren—just those damn lights bouncing in the rearview like warning bells. A door opened, and a shadow stepped out.

My mouth was dry, my palms wet.

I rolled down the window before he even reached me.

"Show me your hands, sir," the voice called.

"Yes, sir," I said, both hands on the wheel, trying to sound older, calmer, more in control than I felt.

He walked up slow, flashlight cutting through the car like a scalpel.

"You know why I stopped you?"

"I wasn't stopped, sir. I, uh... dropped a cigarette. Pulled over to find it."

He didn't say anything right away. Just leaned in and sniffed.

"You been drinking tonight?"

And there it was.

That question.

I had maybe a second to decide whether to lie or lean into the truth and hope the name-dropping worked.

I leaned.

"I was at the city gala," I said. "With Sergeant Moore and some of the council. Just left a bit ago."

He stared at me. Looked down at my license. Then back at me.

"You worked the event?" He finally asked.

"No, sir. I was a guest," I clarified, trying to keep my voice steady.

"Guest?"

"Yes, sir. You can ask Sargent Moore. We drank the same whiskey at the bar."

That part landed hard. I saw it flicker in his eyes—recognition, hesitation, something.

He stepped back from the window.

"You sure you don't want me to follow you home?"

"No, sir. I'm just heading up the mountain. Five minutes out."

He stood there a second longer than I wanted. Then, wordless, he handed me my license.

"Be careful," he warned.

I didn't wait for him to get back to his car. I fired the engine and rolled out, gravel crunching under my tires as I merged back onto the dark road. My heart was hammering, hands shaking on the wheel.

For a second, I looked back.

No movement.

No pursuit.

I exhaled—slow and sharp.

The mountain swallowed me back up like it always had, like it knew I didn't belong anywhere else just yet.

But I also knew I'd just walked a razor-thin line. One wrong word, one bad read on that officer, and I wouldn't just be grounded or lose another party—I could've lost everything. My job. My shot at being the first Raye to graduate. Even the little trust I'd managed to earn with people who actually believed in me. One slip, and I'd be just another Raye story they whispered about on the mountain—drunk, reckless, wasted potential.

This time?

I got lucky.

23

THE FUNNEL

Junior year was on deck, and while that meant getting closer to senior-junior prom—a milestone everyone talked about—it also meant the stress of figuring out who the hell I was taking. By that point, I'd gone on a few dates here and there. Ava and I had our moments working together at Blockbuster, but she had a serious boyfriend, and then she left the store and moved to Georgia. So, that one fizzled out before it could spark.

At this point in my story, I'd rounded all the bases. One girl even went full-on Code Red stalker. She'd randomly show up at places I was, uninvited, sometimes wearing hats and sunglasses, as if she were some undercover agent. She'd creep past my house at night, driving slow to see if my SUV was parked out front. I'm pretty sure if I'd let her, she'd have tossed me in a basement and made me "put the lotion on my skin." I guess I kissed her a little too right. It got real creepy, real quick.

The insecurities were still loud—hell, louder now. I didn't have sports to lean on anymore. On the mountain, you could be ugly and dumb, but if you wore a jersey on Friday night, you had a girl. Maybe two. Without that, I was on my own, but somehow, I managed.

Summer was winding down, and between friends in the Valley and my high school crew, I felt like I was always running—doing stuff I probably shouldn't have been but doing it anyway. Math had started becoming a problem back in 10th grade, and my teacher suggested I put in some work over the summer. I didn't. That would come back to haunt me. Instead, I spent my summer cash on a PlayStation and rented games for free through Blockbuster. Every missed homework problem probably had a game title attached to it.

As the school year loomed, someone came up with the idea to throw one last summer rager at the cabin. We were pros at this point—logistics down to muscle memory. Saxton had even hosted a few without me when I was working or in the Valley. I'll admit, I was starting to like the convenience of restaurants and air-conditioning more than fighting off bugs in the woods, but this was tradition.

That party started like any other. Music bumping. Trucks lined up like a makeshift car show. People from all corners of the county showed up. But then, uninvited guests rolled in— some guys from Sylvania High.

Eagle High and Sylvania had never mixed well. It went back years—trash talk at games, fights in parking lots, even a few county fair scuffles. On our turf, it always felt like they had something to prove, like they came looking for cracks in the rules just to stir things up. That's why we'd made our one rule so clear: **no fighting.**

It was the only way to keep the party train rolling without getting shut down. But with Sylvania boys in the mix, that rule was lucky to last as long as it did. We'd had a few scuffles, even a quick knockout that was probably deserved, but never anything that blew up.

That night, I was dialed in. Buzzed just enough to enjoy it without going over the edge, which was something I had learned with experience. Then one of the Sylvania boys pulled out a beer funnel, and Plug took it and raised that funnel up like we were in a damn arena.

"No one—and I mean no one—can beat Claxton Raye on the funnel!"

A wave of cheers erupted across the party. Some folks banged their fists on the side of the cabin, others clapped their red Solo cups together like tambourines. I just shook my head and laughed—like I didn't love the attention.

Truth was, I'd earned it. I wasn't the fastest runner. Wasn't the starting quarterback. But when it came to slamming beer through a funnel? I was undefeated. It was the one "sport" I'd held onto after walking away from the others. And now, with a crowd pressing in, I had no choice but to show out.

First up, the challenger.

Some cocky kid from Sylvania High stepped up, shirt half unbuttoned, hat turned backwards, gold chain glinting in the cabin lights. I poured his beer for him and handed him the hose. He knocked it back in 4.4 seconds. People gave him a little golf clap. Not bad. But not me.

I raised my brow at Plug, who grinned like the devil and clicked his stopwatch.

"Let's go, champ," Plug said.

The funnel was already loaded. I didn't pour it myself, which I usually did, but I didn't think twice. I was too busy soaking up the moment. The chants started building around me like a drumroll.

"Clax-ton! Clax-ton!"

I tilted my head back, grabbed the hose, and let it rip.

The liquid burned a little going down. Not foam, not cold. Kinda... hot?

3.1 seconds. The crowd lost their damn minds.

I wiped my mouth, grinned, and threw my arms up like a gladiator. High fives flew at me from all angles. Plug jumped on my back. I was the king again.

But then—

It hit.

Not a buzz. Not a wobble. Not that warm beer haze I knew like muscle memory.

Fire.

It started in my throat like someone lit a match inside my esophagus. Then it dropped into my chest, igniting a deep, stabbing heat that spread like wildfire into my gut. My eyes started watering instantly. I couldn't swallow. Couldn't even breathe right.

I staggered away from the crowd, hand out like I was searching for something to hold onto. The corner of the cabin caught me, and I leaned into it, trying to stay upright.

"Claxton?" I heard Saxton's voice behind me, but it was far off, like he was shouting through water.

My knees wobbled. My jaw clenched to keep from crying out. My stomach turned over like I'd swallowed hot gravel.

Then I heard Plug's voice—sharp, alarmed.

"You put what in there?!"

Heads started turning. I looked up, vision blurry from the tears that I was trying to hide, and saw the Sylvania High boys laughing like they'd pulled off the prank of the year. One of them tossed a mason jar onto the ground, glass clinking against a crumpled beer can.

The word "shine" written on painters tape caught the moonlight for just a second, and my heart dropped.

Moonshine.

They'd loaded the funnel with homemade, backwoods rotgut. The clear kind that tasted like jet fuel.

The realization hit harder than the alcohol.

I turned toward Saxton to tell him I didn't feel right, but before I could open my mouth, I buckled forward.

A horrible sound came out of me, somewhere between a cough and a choke. Then something wet hit my shoes.

People stopped. The music didn't. But conversations died.

I dropped to my knees, hand over my mouth.

And then I saw it.

Blood.

Thick, dark, pouring out of me in slow motion. I felt it on my chin, warm and metallic. I wiped my hand across my lips and held it up.

Red. *Everywhere.*

Saxton skidded to a stop beside me. Plug and Jacob froze like someone had hit pause on their bodies. My ears were ringing. My arms were weak.

I was vomiting blood.

I felt hands on me, trying to hold me up, but it all blurred together. My legs were useless. Someone laid me down, and everything tilted sideways. Somehow, I was on a couch. When did we get back to the cabin? A bucket was under my head. Voices echoed in the background. Laughter, shouting, someone cussing about what happened.

A hand rested gently on my back.

"You've been breathing," someone said. "We been taking turns checking."

I wanted to speak, to ask what the hell happened. But I didn't have the strength. My stomach clenched again, dry heaves curling me in half.

'*Why me?*' I thought.

I wasn't the big man on campus. I didn't talk shit. I wasn't chasing their girls.

Why?

I didn't get an answer. Only the taste of iron in my mouth and the weight of knowing—if that shine had been just a little stronger, or I'd funneled a second hit...

I might've died on a cabin floor while the party went on around me.

24
A WARNING HEEDED

The first few weeks of junior year were going pretty well. I had survived that cabin party, somehow, and was back to living the Eagle High life, which for me meant cracking jokes, keeping up the party boy reputation, and making fun of myself before anyone else had the chance.

By that point in high school, there were two tracks: standard and advanced. Advanced was for the so-called "smart kids with a future," while standard was more of a baseline Alabama diploma path. In typical high school fashion, that divide only widened by junior year. The advanced kids had their sights set on college, while the standard track was seen as the slower path—those destined for hourly work and hard hats. I was technically on the advanced path, but there was one subject I couldn't keep up in — math. I ignored it until it was basically too late.

One day, Principal John called me into his office. My junior math teacher was sitting across from him, and neither looked thrilled.

"Claxton," the principal said, "you're going to fail junior

math. We know this because you just bombed the first two assessments that reviewed last year's material. You had a 61 at the end of sophomore year. If you want to graduate, you need to step down to standard and focus on catching up."

Then he hit me with a question that felt foreign—alien even.

"Have you considered college?"

That word had floated around my house a few times growing up, but more like a fantasy than a plan. A joke, almost. Claxton, the first Raye to graduate from high school—imagine if he went to college too! They gave me the weekend to think about it, but I already knew my answer.

I looked at both of them and said it out loud.

"If I want to graduate, I need to switch to standard. I ain't college material anyway. I'm a Raye. I'll work like my daddy and party 'til then."

That decision put me on a quieter road. Some of my buddies started drifting away—they had practice, starters' jerseys, and praise from coaches and crowds. They were taking college-level courses, getting attention. I was just floating, drifting through standard classes with kids I'd never really connected with before.

At my job in the Valley, the crew I started with had mostly moved on. Only Brent and store manager Trish were left from the old days. Even prom—the junior-senior prom in the spring—felt hollow. My prospects with girls were fading fast. Saxton had a new girlfriend, was getting more field time, and had music and school pulling him away, too. I was feeling more and more alone. The jokes I cracked in class felt heavier, like I was trying too hard. Even the teachers didn't laugh anymore.

They just sighed or sent me out.

I told myself it was the stress of growing up. But something about this year—about the silence between the noise—felt different.

By the time the holidays crept up, I was worn out. Mentally done. I had a few moments where that old Raye voice started whispering in my head, low and cold.

"Just quit. Everyone else did. You wouldn't be the first. Sure as hell won't be the last."

Then, one late afternoon near Christmas break, I got invited to hang out by a guy I'd known from junior high. We weren't tight—more like background noise to each other. Same classes sometimes, same parties here and there. His name was Brandon. He was a known stoner, while I mostly stuck to beer and the occasional party circle.

At first, I almost said no. Something about the invite felt off—like one of those moments where your gut whispers, *"Don't go."* But junior year had me worn down, lonely, drifting. I didn't want to sit at home again, staring at walls or at myself in the mirror. So, I shrugged, told myself it was nothing, and said yes because boredom is hell of a salesman. Even as I climbed into his car, a little voice nagged at me: *'This isn't your lane, Claxton.'* I drowned it out and went anyway.

We hopped in his car and started cruising the backroads, talking about nothing and everything, from old teachers to stupid memories to how the rich kids were probably gonna end up as douche doctors in some glass office far from Sand Mountain. I was relaxed at first, but then he turned down a dirt road I'd only heard about in rumors. A place where the really lost kids went. Where the dropouts and the strung-out disappeared into trailers you couldn't find on a map.

It was the kind of place where my uncle had killed a man once.

My stomach twisted. My gut told me to speak up, to say I needed to go home. But I didn't. I just sat there, silent, while we pulled up to a clearing of broken-down mobile homes—rusted, sun-faded, half-sunk into the earth. There were old cars and trucks parked at odd angles, kid toys in the dirt like frozen time bombs. Brandon looked at me and smiled.

"Come on," he said. "Wanna show you something. Something we've been working on—think you can help too."

Inside, the trailer smelled like melted plastic and death. A burn in the back of the throat. Three people were inside—thin, gray-skinned, eyes like lost dogs. One woman, older but not ancient, clung to Brandon like she wanted something more than affection. When he brushed her off, she slithered over to me, wrapped herself around me like a spider, and purred about how "cute" I was, then asked if I brought any cash.

Brandon pulled her away and told her to pour us a drink. I stepped around cracked batteries and pill boxes scattered across the floor. Every surface was cluttered with glass—coffee pots, vases, cracked jars. That smell hit again—like nail polish remover and cat piss combined into something worse.

They handed me a Budweiser, but I didn't touch it. My legs were locked. I just wanted out. Then came Brandon's pitch, all smiles and promise.

Meth.

They were making meth.

And he wanted me to be part of it.

Before I could say anything, someone stirred on the couch

behind us. A gaunt man lifted a glass pipe to his lips, lit it, and exhaled a thick white cloud into the ceiling. He fell back like it was Sunday morning and he'd just been saved.

My body went rigid. My vision narrowed.

"Get out," something screamed in me. *"Get out right **now.**"*

Gunshots cracked through the air outside.

Brandon jumped up to check. I couldn't have been happier for the interruption.

It was his dad—strung out and firing into the woods at nothing.

Brandon hesitated, not wanting to get involved.

"Let's go talk," he said finally.

Back in the car, he talked. I didn't listen. I was replaying every image—every smell, every noise, every face. When he dropped me off, I barely mumbled a goodbye. I got in my car and never looked back.

Brandon dropped out about a month later.

That trailer exploded seven months after I stepped foot inside it.

The people who were there that day? I never saw them again.

As for me?

I went home, took the longest shower of my life, and decided that maybe quitting wasn't the answer after all.

I didn't know it at the time, but that trailer wasn't just a fluke or a freak moment—it was a preview. That drug... it wouldn't stay tucked away in the backwoods forever. In the years to come, it would creep into more lives than the gospel ever could. Quiet at first. Then louder. And then... unstoppable.

It would become a war.

And not everyone would make it out.
That day was my warning.
And I listened.

25
WINTER'S CHILL

Winter had settled over Sand Mountain with the kind of cold that crept into your bones and made every morning feel like climbing out of a frozen coffin. After Christmas break, things slowed down. Ever since the scare at the meth trailer, I kept my head down. No more jokes in class. No more backroad detours. Just school, work, and home. It was the first time in years I'd followed such a tight routine. Even math, my eternal enemy, had started to make sense. I wasn't excelling, but I was trying. That mattered.

But then came the basketball game. Section High—the rival school tucked just across the county line—was hosting, and Eagle High was rolling deep to cheer on our boys. I wasn't playing anymore, hadn't in a while, but I still liked to show up, support, scream at the refs, and pretend I still belonged to that brotherhood. The game was on a Friday, and since my house sat roughly halfway between our school and theirs, I ran home first to shower and change.

As I headed out, I chose the normal route—not the winding backroads, not the hollow with the meth ghosts. Just the usual two-lane path that carried you through the familiar curves of our town, ending at a four-way stop that had, for the last eight or nine years, been nothing more than a blinking light and an old farmer's billboard.

But not today.

The four-way stop was quieter than it had ever been. The sound of my music, of the world spinning around me, seemed to be the only noise in a space that had once been calm. Too calm. Too perfect. A place I thought I could just coast through without a thought. But I was wrong.

I didn't notice them at first—those damn ghosts. Just another day at that intersection. But when I came around the curve, I saw them. Standing there. Six of them. Dressed in those white robes. Hoods over their faces, hiding from the world. It felt like stepping into a time machine and landing somewhere I didn't want to be. 1960. Hell, maybe 1980.

Two cars were in front of me, and the traffic backed up at the stop signs. The world was moving at its own pace while I stood there. And them, just standing there. Handing out pamphlets like they were selling cookies. Smiling. Nodding like they had all the answers.

I didn't want to look at them, but I couldn't stop. They were there. And as soon as I locked eyes with one, I knew what was coming. The words I'd heard a thousand times in my life. But this time, it felt different. This time, it hit me in a way I couldn't ignore.

"Listening to that n***** music is a sin."

The words hung in the air like a slap, like something that physically hit me in the chest. My mind flashed back to Aaliyah, to Ava, to every single one of my friends who'd felt this exact kind of hate on a daily basis. People who, unlike me, didn't have the luxury of ignoring it. They lived with it. They breathed it in with every step, every moment.

I unbuckled my seatbelt. The move was mechanical. Automatic. My hand went for the door before I even realized it, swinging it wide with a force that knocked the guy back a step. I didn't give a damn about the noise or the chaos. My body moved on its own. I was so angry, I didn't even recognize myself.

I grabbed his donation bucket—his offering for hate—and threw it as hard as I could into the woods. The sound of the plastic container smacking the trees behind me was satisfying in a way I couldn't explain. But it wasn't enough. Not nearly.

I grabbed him by the front of his hood, and in one savage motion, I yanked it off. His face—right there in front of me. A face I knew. One I'd seen around town. They always said it wasn't anyone you knew, but of course it was. It always was.

I held that hood up high, fingers clenched around the thick white cloth, and I ripped it. Right through the middle. Right through the eyeholes. I didn't care. It didn't matter what it was made of. I tore it like it had been tearing at me for years. The seams gave way easily, and as I shredded that hood, something inside me snapped.

I screamed.

Not words. Not anything you could really understand. It was pure emotion—anger, hurt, confusion, disgust—rising up from somewhere deep inside. It was the kind of scream that could crack the earth open if you let it. I wasn't just pissed. I was fucking done.

I gave him two birds, the middle fingers straight up in the

air, and let the air between us crack with a silence that felt like a thousand words I couldn't say.

And then I spat on the gravel. Right there. Right at his feet.

I dropped the hood like a bomb on the ground and slammed the door of my SUV with so much force I thought I might break it. The engine roared to life, tires screeching as I sped off, heart hammering in my chest. My hands were shaking. My mind was spinning. I expected a siren to light up behind me at any moment. I expected something to happen.

But nothing did.

Just the music. Just the sound of my tires biting into the asphalt, like nothing in the world mattered anymore. I wasn't a kid anymore. And that intersection wasn't a place I could go through unscathed.

That was the last time I ever saw them in person. The last time I had to look at those assholes in their hoods. But I knew it wouldn't be the last time hate showed up like that.

By the time I reached the school parking lot, my hands were still trembling on the wheel. Every shadow felt like it might hide flashing lights or a hood waiting to follow me in. But nothing came. Just the buzz of the gym lights spilling out into the cold night, pulling me back into the noise of normal life.

The game had already started by the time I got there. I made my way to the student section, where I found the usual crew—non-athletes yelling as if we were courtside coaches. It was easier to watch now. Still painful, knowing I'd walked away from something my family had bled for. But there was a strange peace in the bleachers. No pressure. Just noise and warmth.

And then, just before tip-off, I felt it.

A small presence beside me. Soft. Quiet.

"Can I sit by you?"

I turned and saw her. Big eyes. A hoodie a size too large. Faint scars of something—maybe physical, maybe not—just beneath the surface.

I didn't know her well. All I knew was she was a freshman. Sister of a classmate. She used to play ball herself until her body wouldn't let her anymore.

She smiled gently, like she already knew I'd say yes.

She sat.

And just like that, something shifted.

Her name was Brittany, and her entrance brought something I never expected but desperately needed.

26

UNSPOKEN CONNECTIONS

The senior-junior prom was just around the corner. There was a buzz in the air about who Ryan and I were bringing, as the word spread between the guys. On the surface, everything looked normal—boys speculating, girls preening, everyone waiting for the big night. But deep down, I couldn't shake the feeling that I had made a choice I wasn't entirely happy with. I wished I had the nerve to ask Brittany. She was always on my mind, but I knew it was too late.

The date I had already asked to go with me was from a nearby town called Ider. She was cute, popular, fun, and funny, everything a guy would want in a prom date. She had this big, contagious laugh that made people look her way, and she always showed up to games in the latest clothes, like she'd just stepped out of a magazine. Imagine my surprise at how she was thrilled that I'd asked her, or at least she played it off well if it was fake. I couldn't tell, but she made it seem real, and I wanted to believe it was.

What I didn't understand was why she agreed to go with me, especially considering how much attention she would have gotten if she had gone with someone else. She was the type of girl everyone wanted, and there I was, some quiet, confused guy kind of on the outskirts of the high school scene. But Ryan's girlfriend and prom date had gone to school with her, so we were all familiar, and we had gotten to know each other through them.

People asked, "How the hell did he pull this off?"

And truthfully, I wondered the same thing sometimes. She was beautiful, and I was... well, *me.* But we were friends, and I thought that was enough. I told myself to be excited about the date, about her.

The guys at school, the seniors especially, were way more excited about her going with me than they were about seeing me at prom. They all made jokes and commented about how lucky I was, but inside, I just felt like an imposter. She and I shared a few laughs, and we became friendly before, during, and after prom. But no matter how much fun we had together, Brittany was always there in the back of my mind, gnawing at me. I couldn't push her out even though I tried.

After that night at the basketball game, me and Brittany didn't suddenly become inseparable, but little moments kept stacking up. Passing each other in the hallway. A quick comment that turned into a real conversation. By the time spring rolled around, it felt natural to look for her between classes, like my day was missing something if we didn't cross paths.

It was always casual, but underneath it, there was this quiet connection. Almost like a secret. She had this way of making me feel like she was the only one who understood.

Brittany wasn't flashy—long brown hair that she often tucked into a hoodie, wide brown/hazel-like eyes that seemed to see past whatever mask you put up. She carried herself with a kind of quiet strength that didn't need to be announced.

The strangest thing about it all was how little Brittany mentioned her condition—her cancer. She never complained. She never let on that she was struggling. It was like it wasn't even a part of her life, despite it being a part of all our lives. Sometimes she'd say, "Good day" or "Okay day," and it took me a while to learn what those really meant. The way she said it was so soft, so careful.

I'd vent to her about the things that had been bothering me, things that seemed trivial in comparison to what she was going through. I wasn't sure why she wanted to listen. But she did. She listened like it was the most important thing in the world, and when she spoke, her advice was always soft, precise, and so welcoming, like a warm light in the dark.

I found myself apologizing one day, mid-conversation, the kind of moment when everything feels like it's building up to something. It was between classes, and I knew I had to say it, to admit what I'd been carrying.

"I'm sorry," I told her, "for not asking you to prom."

Her smile was small but genuine. It was the kind of smile that didn't show sadness, but rather the quiet strength she carried with her, the kind of smile that always made me feel like I didn't need to apologize at all.

"I hope to experience it one day," she said, her voice as calm and certain as always, but there was something deeper in her words that I couldn't place. A kind of quiet wisdom that made my chest tighten. She didn't say anything more, but in that moment, I knew she wasn't just talking about prom.

It was that same kind of wisdom that I had felt when I was

with her, even though we never really spoke about it. She was dealing with something I couldn't understand, but still, she found a way to show up. And I wanted to do the same, but I wasn't sure how.

Even after the night of prom came and went, and I'd done what I thought was right by bringing the girl from Ider, Brittany stayed with me. Her absence at that big event weighed more than I had anticipated. It was like a shadow that clung to everything, never letting go.

And it wasn't until much later that I realized—what she had meant to me, what we had, it wasn't just about high school, or prom, or any of the small things we'd shared. It was bigger. Brittany had been a part of me long before I ever understood it. I didn't know it yet, but she was about to become even more central to everything I had to face.

27

SENIOR YEAR SHADOWS

The summer before my senior year slipped past like smoke through my fingers. I missed more parties than I made it to, but by then, the draw of bonfires in the woods and half-drunk conversations under a canopy of stars had lost its magic. I wasn't the same anymore. The things that used to pull me in just didn't hold weight. Instead, I spent my free time with older friends who'd already graduated, most of them folks I knew through work.

While the rest of my class buzzed with excitement—preparing to claim their senior crown, planning each football Friday and spirit week down to a science—I found myself slipping into the silence between their plans. I wasn't exactly dreading senior year. But the "what comes next" had started pressing down on me like a cinderblock on my chest.

I had passed junior year math by a thin hair, but it had taken everything in me. Every late-night cram session, every half-understood lesson, every minute spent pretending I had it together—it wore me down. And unlike a lot of my classmates, I was entering uncharted territory. My brother never made it through senior year. One cousin dropped out before the end of his junior fall semester. The Raye boys didn't exactly have a history of walking across that stage.

The wealthier kids were already taking trips to campuses across the South—touring Auburn, Alabama, Tennessee, etc. Some of them already had scholarships rolling in. They posted their acceptance letters like trophies, and their parents bragged about legacy status and academic achievement like it was a family tradition. Me? I hadn't applied anywhere.

A handful of my friends were eyeing the junior college nearby. It had grown a lot in recent years—offering two-year degrees in everything from nursing to HVAC to education. It was affordable and realistic, and that alone made it a damn good option. For my family, the idea of me going to a four-year university felt like trying to catch a lightning bolt in a jar. We just didn't have the money. Dad had done everything he could after getting laid off from the aluminum plant, and he eventually landed a janitor position at a technical school in the Valley. It was a massive pay cut, but the benefits were solid, and the retirement would carry him through.

And true to form, my old man didn't sulk about it. He didn't bitch or drag his feet. He became the best damn janitor that county had ever seen—same work ethic, same grit, just a different uniform. No more swing shifts meant his hours were more manageable, and at his age, that mattered. Still, I saw the toll it took.

Brittany had gotten sick again during the summer. Being in the hospital for a stretch. I knew from our conversations that these stints came and went—like storms rolling in, tearing through her body and then fading. She always came back just as calm, just as composed, just as cool as ever. I never saw her complain. Not once. When we talked on the phone, or when I'd catch her around town, she wouldn't bring it up unless I asked. And even then, she'd just shrug, smile softly, and say something like, "It was an okay day," or "I'm glad to be out."

She never let the focus stay on her for long. Brittany had this way—like a spotlight she refused to step into. Always turning it around, always asking about me instead. And not just in a polite, surface-level way. She genuinely wanted to know how I was doing, what I was planning. She'd listen to my half-baked dreams and doubts and remind me, gently but firmly, to keep pushing.

"You're better than you think," she told me once. "Just gotta start believing it."

She gave advice like someone twice her age—soft, precise, steady. Like a scalpel, not a hammer. I didn't realize how much I leaned on her voice in my head until one afternoon, after she'd come home from a check-up, she flipped the script. Instead of listening, she opened up.

She talked about her own future.

Graduation. College. A major in the medical field, maybe. "I want to help people the way they helped me," she explained.

She spoke of marriage one day, but made it clear she wouldn't let anything interfere with her goals. She had it all mapped out, like she'd been practicing the speech in her head for years.

And then, out of nowhere, she brought up Brent.

"You ever talk to Brent about the theater program?" she asked. "At the junior college?"

I blinked. I'd forgotten I even mentioned Brent to her. But, of course, she remembered. I had told her once that Brent, an old friend, did some acting and tech work for the junior college plays. And that they offered scholarships.

"You said you liked storytelling," she continued. "There's more than one way to tell a story, you know."

It was the nudge I didn't know I needed. And Brittany never asked for credit. Never made it about her. She just lit the path and stepped back into the shadows.

The next day, I drove out to Brent's place.

"Think I could act well enough to get a scholarship?" I asked.

He laughed at first, like I was joking. Then his face changed.

"There's more than just acting, you know," he stated. "Theater ain't just the stage. Most of it's behind the curtain. But yeah, if you're serious, go down there Wednesday night. Ask for Mr. Webb."

So, I did.

I pulled up to the theater building, bigger than I expected, with no clue where to enter. I followed someone through a side door and stepped into a world I'd never seen before. The place buzzed like an anthill kicked open—people moving props, setting lights, adjusting costumes. On stage, a few folks rehearsed lines. Others moved in and out of dressing rooms. Then a man raised his hand, and everything stopped.

Mr. Webb. The one Brent told me about. He looked like he ran the place with pure electricity.

I walked up, heart pounding, and said, "Sir, I was told you might be able to help. I'm interested in trying out for a theater scholarship."

He didn't hesitate.

He reached into his toolbelt, handed me a drill and a handful of screws.

"Can you use these?"

"Yes, sir," I replied.

"You know how to build stairs from that wood over there?"

I looked and calculated quickly.

"I can, but I'll need to measure the space first. If I just build something without knowing the height or width, it might not fit," I answered.

He grinned.

"Right answer. Go figure it out. Come see me when you've got something solid."

I spent the next three hours building those stairs. Talking to the crew. Learning about the set for *The Wizard of Oz*. Watching how Webb worked, how the cast moved, how every small part mattered.

I came back the next practice night. Then again, and again. I wasn't promised anything, but I kept showing up.

I filled out an application. Paid the small fee out of pocket. I wasn't expecting much, but for the first time, I had something to chase. Something that felt like mine.

Still, I kept other options in my back pocket—plant jobs, trade school, a possible promotion at Blockbuster, even starting at Walmart and working my way up. Because senior year had arrived, and it wasn't going to wait for me to figure it all out.

But maybe, just maybe, I didn't have to have all the answers yet.

Maybe believing I could find them was enough—for now.

And if I ever forgot, Brittany would remind me.

Because even as she battled for her life, she never stopped

fighting for others and watching her do that forced me to stop selling myself short. If she could carry her battles with grace and still push me toward something better, then I had no excuse to quit on myself. Her resilience didn't just steady me— it gave me a blueprint. I couldn't control where I came from, but I could decide what came next.

28
RIVALRY AND RAGE

The first few months of senior year went by smooth enough. The first block PE turned into mostly just sitting in the gym, playing Rook and poker, or risking the chance of being caught out at the ag shop or laughing at underclassmen in their classes. Rook was my go-to if I wasn't out back building or cooking something during those early hours. Block two—teacher's aid—meant janitor duties for Principal John. Things like weed-eating the school grounds, mopping floors, helping set up pep rallies, or folding chairs for meetings—anything physical that kept me too tired to cause trouble. That was his plan, and I played along. By the time I hit English and Science in the afternoon, I was already dragging.

Fall and winter kept the seniors grounded. We didn't skip as much since cold creeks and rivers made hiding out less tempting. My interactions with Brittany were steady—friendly, sometimes flirty—but unless I missed a giant neon sign (which wouldn't be the first time), I never felt like she wanted something more. She was the sweet sophomore with a heart everyone adored. I was the senior with the rep and a list of strikes. She was better than me in every way that counted.

First semester flew by, and for me, that meant one thing—math. And the looming scholarship decisions from the junior college. Most of my crew already had plans. Jacob snagged a football scholarship to a school in Tennessee. Ryan and Percy were heading to Huntsville for engineering. Susan—yeah, the same girl who was my first love back in elementary school—had landed a teaching scholarship to Bama. Others had acceptance letters in hand, scattered across Alabama.

Me? I shrugged when asked what came next. Folks knew the Raye name didn't come with diplomas. It came with factory jobs, alcoholism, bad backs, and mugshots. Dropouts. Junkies. Survivors who barely made ends meet. But something buzzed different this year. It wasn't pressure to score touchdowns anymore—it was pressure to walk that stage on graduation night. All I had to do was keep my head down and pass math.

Problem was... Football season hits hard in small-town Alabama, especially when rivalry week rolls in. Sylvania week. The same school where a few of their own were behind the moonshine stunt that nearly killed me. That poison they called a joke. That memory? Still burning.

Friday night. Game night. The air hung thick with Southern tension. A mild, humid fog blanketed the field like a ghost refusing to leave. Both stands were packed. School colors everywhere. Face paint. Pom-poms. Horns. Parents wearing faded letterman jackets from decades prior. The energy was raw and feral.

Both teams were locked in a defensive slugfest. No big plays—just hard hits, helmet pops echoing like shotgun blasts, and trash talk so thick you could see it float between facemasks.

It wasn't just a game. It was a powder keg.

Around the restrooms and concession stands, students from both sides mingled, circling like coyotes. Parents started lobbing insults over dirty hits. Teachers tried to keep the peace, but the slow burn was obvious. This wasn't staying on the field.

The third quarter was winding down when it ignited. In the visiting student section, three beer funnels popped up—bright red Solo-cupped towers being passed like torches. It was subtle to the adults, but every student there knew. It was a reference to that night. A taunt. A shot fired.

Then came the hit. A Sylvania linebacker—number 44— laid Perry out with a cheap shot two yards out of bounds, right in front of our student section. The kid stood up, grinning, and gave a mocking funnel-chug motion followed by a casual wave like he was thanking us for the memory. A flag flew on the field, but nothing flagged what came next.

At the restrooms, a parent from our side and one from theirs exchanged words that didn't stay words for long. A push. A scream. Then chaos.

Students from the visiting side began rushing toward the front of their stands. You could feel it—war drums in your chest. Our side responded, from freshmen to seniors, moving like a single stormfront.

And Barney Fife—our lone cop—was facing the wrong direction, caught in the parent brawl.

I started pushing my way out of the bleachers. Brittany reached out and caught my hand, stopping me just long enough for our eyes to lock. "Claxton..." she whispered.

I looked at her, gave the softest smile I could muster, and mouthed, "Sorry." Then turned and sprinted.

It was tribal. It was ancient. Screams and sneakers on bleachers, fists in the air. Our crowd poured into theirs. The field didn't matter anymore.

I weaved through the chaos, dodging a punch thrown wide, eyes searching for that face—his face. The one who had poured the shine into the funnel that night, laughing while I nearly bled out in front of my friends. And there he was, smirking like it was all still a joke. That was who I wanted. That was who I had to reach.

I made a beeline through the crowd, heart pounding like a war drum, until I got within reach. Principal John and the faculty were trying to pull kids apart—but I got through, wound my right arm with everything God ever gave me, and dropped that sorry bastard like a sack of wet cement. He hit the ground hard, eyes rolling.

Instantly, pain burst in my back twice. I turned to find another Sylvania player, still in full pads, his buddy from the funnel night flanking him.

I snapped. All instinct. I charged, no pads, no helmet—just rage. I was ready to send the guy through a wall. But I never got there.

Principal John—like some divine linebacker—lifted me from behind and dragged me away, dropped me down like a sack of potatoes a few feet from the melee. I was catching my breath, rage shaking in my fingertips, when I heard it:

"Funnel more moonshine, n****r lover!"

That was it.

There was no stopping me now. No holding me back. I tore toward the Sylvania player, ripped off his helmet mid-sentence, and used it like a hatchet, splitting his nose open with a crack that silenced everything. Blood sprayed like red mist. Gasps. Screams. And the click of handcuffs.

Barney finally found me.

Just like a Raye. Face-down in handcuffs as the fog thickened and the Friday night lights burned above.

And I knew... Monday was coming like judgment.

29

LAST SHOT

Our lovely local cop released me to my parents that night, only after the parents of the Sylvania boy I throttled finally agreed that I meant no harm. I wasn't trying to kill him—but it was nice to see blood for blood. The game was suspended. That buzzing Friday night tension didn't end with a final whistle; it ended with a siren.

Then came Monday morning. I found myself in Principal John's office, flanked by my mom and dad. Principal John sat down with a calm but irritated look on his face. He didn't even greet us—just looked at my folks and said, "He can stay and finish the last few months of his senior year."

Then he asked to speak with me alone.

My dad stood, shook his hand, and gave me that look—stern and silent, the kind of look that promised pain if I screwed this up again. They left, and I stayed, head down, waiting for a sound, anything.

Principal John sighed, leaned back in his chair, and quietly said, "I was the only one."

He paused.

"The only one who voted for you to stay and finish your school career here."

Another pause.

"All other high school teachers said no. All of them. After twelve and a half years, they wanted you gone. You would've had to finish down the road somewhere or try to get homeschooled. No walking across that field at graduation. Probably would've hurt your shot at college, too."

He sat forward then, serious, measured.

"I said no. Because I heard what that boy said. It was wrong. It was old-school hate. It was everything that's wrong with the world. But your reaction? That's what he wanted. He won, Claxton. You bled him, but he beat you. You let hate pull you off course."

His voice cracked a little, emotion tucked in the corners.

"Winning is smiling in the face of that kind of ugliness and going on with your life. That's what breaks them. But you gave him what he wanted. Wherever he is right now, whoever raised him to think like that, they're probably proud of him. Because you reacted."

He let that hang, and I let it land.

"This is your last shot. Four and a half more months and math. For teacher's aide, you'll sit in my office and do nothing but math. That's your punishment for now. And whatever else I can think of."

He didn't smile. He didn't have to. I nodded, stood, and walked out into a hallway where I wasn't wanted anymore—at least not by the teachers.

The students who'd cheered and fought beside me Friday night pulled back, reserved and scared to associate with me, afraid they'd be dragged down too. No one thought I'd survive the remainder of my senior year.

Except for one sophomore girl. While everyone else kept their distance, Brittany still waved to me in the halls, still stopped in the halls to talk, still treated me like I wasn't toxic. It gave me the strength to keep pushing forward, and I needed that strength as I tackled math head on.

I stared at the numbers until they blurred. Fractions and equations that made sense to everyone else just mocked me. Every wrong answer felt like another nail in the coffin of my senior year. But when one problem finally clicked—just one— my chest filled with a kind of pride I hadn't felt in months. I thought, *'Maybe I could do this. Maybe.'*

Christmas break came and went. When January rolled around, I kept my head down and my book up. Teachers had ears to the ground, squashing any lingering tensions from the fight. The Sylvania principal and administration visited and apologized. We didn't see those kids again.

But it wouldn't be the last time I'd encounter some of them.

The spring semester meant the final stretch. I was holding out hope for that junior college opportunity, still battling math nightmares, thinking about senior skip day and prom.

Amidst all my math woes, Brittany and I hadn't missed a chance to talk. We were constant. I hadn't even considered anything more than friendship until one random January morning. Ryan and I were killing time before first bell. He was bragging about his girlfriend and asked why I hadn't dated anyone lately—not even one of my coworkers from the store.

I shrugged and told him, "Got a lot going on. Don't need the stress."

He laughed. "Have you told Brittany that?"

I blinked, asking, "Told her what?"

He grinned and replied, "Come on, man. You two are like two little kids scared to ask each other out. She likes you. So, what are you doing? When are you going to ask her to prom?"

Prom. Damn. That was coming up. But Brittany? Would she go? Could she? Would her brother let her? Would her parents?

I spent the next few weeks dropping subtle hints, testing the waters. Then, one day in the hallway, she stopped me. Not normal. She looked at me with those bright eyes and asked flatly:

"So, who are you taking to prom?"

I turned beet red, stuttering like a seventh grader, and somehow choked out, "You... if you'll let me."

She smiled, wide and knowing. "I thought you were never going to ask. But yes, I'll go. I just need to make sure my parents are okay with it first. So, can I tell them now that you asked me, finally?"

I hugged her. "Yes. Please do."

A few days later, she came to me, bubbly as I'd ever seen her, and said her parents gave their blessing. She'd be going dress shopping soon. She'd let me know the colors.

To get your prom ticket, you pay in advance and write your name and your date's name on the teacher's file. I wrote hers proudly, handed over the cash. What I didn't expect was the reaction.

My teacher hugged me. She cried. Other teachers started speaking to me again, smiling, patting me on the back.

Some thought it was a stunt to get back in their good graces. Looking back, it's sad how calculated some people assumed it to be. But at the time, I was just excited.

Yes, Brittany was sick. She had a rare form of cancer. But she was winning. Her attitude, her strength, her care for everyone around her—this wasn't going to beat her. I believed that. We all did.

The next few weeks fell into a rhythm: studying in Principal John's office, surviving math class, helping my old kindergarten teacher, working nights when I could. I didn't party. Even though Saxton was throwing hellraisers down the holler, I stayed home.

It wasn't just about walking across that stage. If I blew this chance, I'd lose everything I'd fought for 12 years to become, maybe even my parents' faith in me. Junior college would be gone. And worse—I'd have to live with the thought that everyone was right about me all along: nothing but a troublemaker who couldn't finish what he started. Just another Raye washed out and stuck. I couldn't afford to blow this shot.

I was moving forward. Slowly. Tiredly. But still moving.

30

PROM NIGHT MAGIC

As the days ticked off the schedule, I inched closer to the finish line. Holding strong around a high D/low C in math class, keeping my nose clean, and sticking to the routine—school, work, home, repeat—was starting to drive me insane. I made appearances at some of the remaining football and basketball games. Though if tensions rose, I'd retreat to calmer spaces, often catching a quiet moment chatting with Brittany if she was around.

Senior skip day rolled around. Some of the seniors took a trip up to the Chattanooga mall. Me? I found myself back at the coal mine with some friends, soaking up the sun and letting the cold water ground me. That cliffside had become something of a sacred spot over the years—a place for thrill, laughter, and reflection. We'd run that beaten-down path to the edge and launch ourselves off, counting the seconds before we smacked into the water below. Some even climbed the trees growing on the edge to get a few more feet of free-fall. It was raw and real.

When you weren't jumping, you lounged at the bottom, on the rocks, catching your breath before either pulling yourself up with the rope or swimming to the trail and hiking back around. Some kids grew up on backyard pools. But me? I had the coal mine. Saxton and I stumbled on it years ago, and it stuck. Crystal-clear water, full of life, but so deep you couldn't touch or see the bottom.

Later on, that depth came in handy when a friend's beat-up car was worth less than what he owed on it. Let's just say the coal mine took care of it.

I sat on the corner of that cliff watching the friends I'd known since elementary school—some I'd only grown close to freshman year—laughing, jumping, splashing. It hit me that this might be one of the last times we were all this carefree. The clock was running out. I thought back to the days of getting paddled daily in elementary school. Never would've guessed I'd end up here, soaking in the last golden hours of our wild, tangled youth.

We swapped stories—the beer runs, the 4-way incident, the fight at the game, cabin parties, field parties, the wins and losses. A full day of nostalgia. We all knew things were changing, but not today.

That night, several of us met at a backwoods burger joint known for its greasy perfection and thick shakes. Some brought their significant others; a few were from Eagle, while others were from elsewhere. Brittany's brother brought her out that night. I don't know if he did it for her or for me, but either way, I was grateful. It was our first outing together outside of school events.

We ate, talked, and laughed. For one night, none of us worried about the past or future. No parties, no booze, just honest joy and a quiet knowing that something good was slipping through our fingers.

That night at the burger joint was our last normal outing before the big dance. After that, every conversation seemed to circle back to prom—what we'd wear, who was going with who, and how fast the year was closing in. People were buzzing with talk of prom as it inched closer and closer, and I was ready for the night and what came with it.

Prom night hit like something out of a movie I never imagined myself in. It wasn't just a dance. It was a turning point, a slow exhale after a year of holding my breath.

Brittany looked stunning that night—so stunning, in fact, that I lost my words for a second when I pulled up in the driveway. Her dress caught the porch light like it had been dipped in starlight, soft blues and silvers that complemented her skin and made her eyes even brighter. Her hair was curled just right, her makeup light and natural—just enough to highlight her beauty without trying to hide a single feature.

We stood there awkwardly for pictures—her mom and mine calling out directions, trying to capture angles we didn't care about. But when we got in the car, away from the flashes and formalities, she was quiet. Nervous. Not her usual bubbly self.

It wasn't until I started the SUV and The Black Crowes came through the speakers with "Hard to Handle" that she finally let out a laugh.

"What?" I asked, glancing over.

She shook her head, still smiling, and said, "That song is the perfect theme for your high school life. Wild. Loud. Unapologetic."

I couldn't help but laugh, too. I hadn't thought about it

that way, but she was dead on. That drive down her winding driveway felt different—like we were leaving one world and entering another.

We met Saxton, Ryan, and their dates at Longhorn in Chattanooga for dinner. We caught some stares—the rough-edged boys from Eagle dressed up like we didn't belong, but laughing and eating like we owned the place. There was a comfort to it, even if we knew the town didn't know what to make of us.

When we arrived at the prom venue, the lights spilled out into the evening air like something magical was happening inside. The line to be announced stretched long, seniors and their dates lined up in nervous, excited pairs. Brittany held my arm tighter than usual, and just before we stepped through the entry arch, she leaned in and whispered, "Just... be ready."

I looked at her, confused, but she just nodded toward the entrance as the principal announced:

"Claxton Raye... and Brittany Carson."

The room erupted.

Not just polite applause, but a roar. Cheering. Whistling. Applause that felt like something much more than high school pageantry. It caught me off guard. I turned to look at Brittany, who had her head slightly down, a soft smile playing on her lips.

I realized then that the cheer wasn't for me. It was for her. For her fight. For her spirit. For being there. I held her hand up like we had just won something, letting her soak in every decibel of it.

The rest of the night was a blur of music and movement. Songs like NSYNC's "Bye Bye Bye", Pink's "Get the Party Started",

Nelly's "Hot in Herre", and even an edited version of Juvenile's "Back That Thang Up" played as the perfect soundtrack for the night. We danced. We laughed. I watched Brittany move like she hadn't a care in the world, and for the first time in a long time, I believed she didn't.

But it was the last slow song of the night that'll stay with me forever.

Lee Ann Womack's "I Hope You Dance" came on, and the room shifted. The chatter died down. The seniors moved close. And when I wrapped my arms around Brittany, she gently laid her head on my chest. She didn't say anything. Didn't have to. Her silence was louder than anything I'd heard that night.

It was a goodbye of sorts. A moment sealed in time. A promise and a plea, all wrapped up in that lean against my chest.

When the song ended, the lights came up, and reality crept back in. Students trickled out in groups, buzzing about afterparties. Brittany and I lingered a moment longer before stepping outside, the cool night air meeting us like a curtain closing on the scene.

The ride home was quiet. The night air through the cracked windows, her hand in mine. Slower music playing. No more nerves. No more performance. Just a stillness between us that felt safe and heavy in all the best ways.

When we pulled into her driveway, we both hesitated. The porch light was on. The night was ending.

She leaned in and gave me a soft, quick kiss, with her lips barely brushing mine. Then she held me in a long, quiet hug that said everything she hadn't said in words. I didn't want to let go. I don't think she did either.

When I drove away, I didn't turn the radio on. Just let the night settle in my bones. That prom wasn't just a dance. It was the moment everything became real—how fragile time is, how precious people are, and how the smallest gestures, like a head on a chest, can echo in your memory forever.

31

THE LAST BELL

With prom behind us, there was only one more hurdle left to celebrate: graduation night. We had five weeks to go, still riding high from the beauty that prom was. Some of us got the news we'd been hoping for—scholarship announcements rolled in like long-awaited rain. And my prayers? They were answered. A two-year theater scholarship to the junior college. First in my family.

All I had to do was pass two more math tests, and I'd be on track to receive that elusive diploma that had dodged every other Raye before me. Test days came and went, and the result: two high Cs. Just enough. Leonard Claxton Raye was going to be an Eagle High School graduate. An alumnus. A damn miracle.

My family buzzed with excitement. Gifts came in from every direction—from every family member still kicking. And not only was I graduating, but I was going to college. Unbelievable.

I celebrated the only way I knew how, the Raye style. We threw a party in the Valley with the Blockbuster crew. Brent and I toasted with whatever we could find, celebrating the fact that we'd both be attending junior college together. He'd decided to go back to school, too, and by some twist of fate, was also on a theater scholarship.

The night before graduation, my dad knocked on my door. He stepped in slow, leaned on the frame, and said, "Look, son, I know you're gonna drink tonight. Just... if you can't drive, call me. I'll come get you." It wasn't a warning. It was a dad's way of saying, *"I'm proud of you."* And it landed.

Then came the day. Some underclassmen cried in the hallways as we walked through the school for the last time. We all came in, even though classes were done and we had nothing left to do. Some of us rode the bus in just for the ritual. We wandered those familiar halls—elementary to junior high to high school—laughing, hugging, lingering. When we walked out that back door together, we weren't students anymore.

That evening, we returned for the ceremony, the sun dropping low, casting long shadows across the football field. We lined up in the hallway, ready to walk across the road toward the stadium. The home stands were filling up—parents, grandparents, cousins, neighbors. All of Sand Mountain was out there, clapping and calling names, waiting.

We stood there in our caps and gowns, looking at each other like we'd all just woken up in someone else's dream. Tears came fast. The weight of it all hit like thunder. We made it. I made it.

Principal John stepped up for one last address. "The booklets I'll hand you are empty. Your real diplomas come after this is done. Please be safe tonight. Congratulations. Be proud of what you've done. I love you all." And then he was gone, walking out into the light.

One by one, names were called. Some kids handed him

condoms, some came across with wet hands, some got fancy with inside jokes. Then it happened.

"Leonard Claxton Raye."

Silence. You could hear a pin drop.

I stood slowly, feeling a thousand eyes lock in on me. There I was, the kid who never thought he'd make it, walking across that field. And in that second, the whole damn story caught up to me—every mistake, every skipped class, every backroad night and broken rule. The full weight of the moment came, emotions surged and disappeared in waves, from my last morning walking those familiar halls to being under the stadium lights in my cap and gown. I floated across that grass like I had ghosts trailing me. Ghosts with the Raye name. Ghosts that never got this far. I was the first. The only. I had made my family proud.

I locked eyes with Principal John. He was grinning. He knew something was coming. He just didn't know what.

I reached for his hand, then dipped him like a dancing partner, clean and smooth, and planted a kiss right on his cheek. Laughter cracked across the stands like fireworks. Flashbulbs burst. The whole crowd rose up. For once, the laughter wasn't at my expense; I got the last laugh, and this time, a standing ovation. I grabbed that empty diploma like it was holy and held it to the sky, fist pumping, hands up, grinning like the damn fool I was.

And then I saw her. Brittany. Standing in the stands, glowing, waving, smiling soft like only she could. I nodded to her—silent thanks for believing in me when I didn't believe in myself.

As I walked back to my seat, everything slowed down.

My boots sank into the grass, the lights buzzed above, and it felt like I was stepping out of one life and into the next. My classmates slapped my shoulder, whispered jokes, wiped tears, and all that noise and nostalgia that comes with graduating. I didn't say a word. I just breathed it all in.

We finished. Tassels turned. We circled up and threw our hats so high they nearly scraped the moon.

Afterwards, family and friends rushed onto the field. Pictures. Hugs. Ugly cries. We laughed until our stomachs hurt. Eventually, we filtered back into the building to collect our real diplomas.

Principal John gave me a mock glare when I approached.

"You know I oughta keep this after that stunt," he threatened. But he handed it over anyway, pulled me in for a hug, and said, "Go do big things, Claxton."

That night, we partied. Some sipped and split. Some got blackout drunk. Some snuck off into dark corners or smoky cars. But me? I took it slow. I soaked it all in. Every laugh, every cheer, every slurred goodbye.

When I finally made it home, Dad was waiting by the back door. He patted me on the back without a word. Just a look that said everything.

I went to bed with my diploma on the nightstand and future plans circling my mind.

In two days, we were leaving for Panama City. And that party... well, that was gonna make everything else look like child's play.

32

CHAOS AT THE CHATEAU

Around 20 of us graduates from Eagle High School were off to spend a few days in Panama City, Florida, for the senior trip. Graduated seniors from all over the U.S. flock to a beach somewhere, and based on the money you have, that could mean a cruise, a beach in Mexico or the Caribbean, or somewhere along the Alabama and Florida Gulf Coast. I was barely able to scrape together the funds to split a room with three other friends, but we made it happen. Our destination: The Chateau—a name that meant nothing to me until we got there and saw it in all its chaotic glory.

We packed our friend's car to the brim and hit the road early Monday morning, just a few days after graduation. Some classmates had already arrived on Sunday, but we were coming in late. The drive was supposed to be full of hype and laughter, a rolling celebration on wheels. But after the first hour on the road, the car fell deathly silent. My companions, full of graduation fatigue and fast food, were soon slumped over, mouths open, snoring like they'd never heard the word "excitement" in their lives.

That left me—white-knuckling the wheel, trying to keep my eyes open as the highway stretched on like some eternal gray ribbon. The exhaustion hit me like a hammer. Graduation, the partying, the planning, the packing—it had all been go-go-go. Now, it was just me, the hum of tires, the static of the radio, and the loud rhythmic breathing of the two dead asleep next to me. I cracked the window, cranked the volume, slapped my own face a couple of times. Nothing was cutting it. My head began to bob, and the lines on the road blurred.

Then it happened.

A horn—long and angry—snapped me back.

I gasped and jerked the wheel. I was in the median, flying past trees and grass, just outside of Enterprise, Alabama. I had fallen asleep at the wheel. Somehow, by pure luck or grace or both, I hadn't drifted into oncoming traffic. I yanked the car back into the southbound lane, my heart thundering in my chest. My hands were trembling as I clutched the wheel. The other drivers stared as we passed—wide-eyed, wondering what kind of circus was going on inside our car.

As I tried to calm my racing pulse, the guys started to stir in the back seat.

One rubbed his eyes, yawned like a toddler, and said, "Hey man, where are we? You good? Need a break?"

I looked at him, my mind still spinning from the fact that I'd just narrowly dodged death, and all I could say was, "Yeah... yeah, I think I do."

We pulled off at the next gas station. I stood outside the car for a long minute, breathing deep and trying to stop shaking. They had no clue what had just almost happened.

The rest of the ride, I gripped the wheel tighter than ever, every set of cars in the opposite lane a reminder of how close I'd come. I didn't turn the music back on until we neared the location. I didn't tell them either—not then, not later. Some things feel too big to share in the moment. Instead, I carried it quiet, the what-ifs chasing me all the way to the coast.

When we finally hit Thomas Drive and saw the strip, it was like crossing into another world. The energy hit us like heat from a furnace. Teens and college kids lined the sidewalks, half-dressed and buzzing, some yelling from balconies, others dancing in truck beds. Every hotel was lit up, every parking lot a beach party in progress. Music blasted from every direction— rap, country, punk, beach house techno, and the bass seemed to make the concrete vibrate beneath our feet.

We rolled up to The Chateau, which looked like a place stuck somewhere between a frat house and a war zone. People were hanging over railings with drinks in hand, barefoot and sunburned, tossing beads, pouring beer into mouths from balconies above. A couple of guys were wrestling in the sand just beside the parking lot, and two girls ran by us, laughing and holding bottles wrapped in towels. We were barely parked before some random dude with a foam cooler asked if we wanted Jell-O shots. No ID checks, no rules, just chaos.

We grabbed our bags and headed to the room—beachfront, third floor. As we walked in, I spotted Ryan and his girlfriend over by the little convenience store that was practically part of the hotel itself. They were already in party mode, red Solo cups in hand, eyes glassy.

We changed into our beach gear, tossed everything else onto the beds, and that was the last time I saw that room until the following afternoon, before dinner. The sand, the lights, the chaos—it all swallowed us whole.

This was no mountain party, no backwoods bonfire. This was something else. This was the wildest rite of passage I'd ever seen.

And we had just arrived.

33
CLUB LA VELA

No cell phone, no way to check in with home—but I had what I thought mattered more: a fake ID. Before our departure, I had obtained a fake ID—just in case it would be harder to buy alcohol down there than it had been up on the mountain. Down here, freedom wasn't about being reachable. It was about being old enough to get into the places we weren't supposed to be. There was something to get into around every corner.

Some of us rented scooters that first day, which were faster than walking and fun until they weren't. One guy got cuffed and later released for drunkenly trying to off-road his scooter through a ditch. Another crashed into the back of a car, slid across the asphalt like a mop rag, and spent the rest of the trip trying to hide the road rash with makeup. We drove those scooters for miles—to dinner, to bars, to wherever the crowd flowed. I vaguely remember eating once or twice—probably dinner, maybe breakfast—but it was mostly alcohol and empty carbs fueling us those days.

One night, we dressed in our finest polos, cargo shorts, and sundresses, ready for Club La Vela—the biggest club in the country back then. Nappy Roots was performing that night. I'd been to the club before during daylight hours, where it was still wild: thousands of teenagers dancing in pools, foam rooms, laser shows, music blasting from every level. But at night? Whole different beast. The line wrapped around the block, but they kept the booze flowing even while you waited. That night, we got lucky—only a 30-minute wait.

I got in with the fake ID. The others weren't so lucky. Once inside, I snuck out drinks for the crew as best I could. Every time I was handed cash, I took a shot for myself. At the time, it seemed like a brilliant plan—free booze, endless fun. But the math caught up with me fast.

Sometime near the start of the concert, we got separated in the chaos. I was drunk, soaked, alone—but it didn't matter. I was right up front, rapping along with Nappy Roots to "Awnaw" and "Po Folks" like I was part of the band. After the set, the members jumped into the crowd, and I somehow ended up doing shots at the poolside bar with Fish Scales from the group.

Somewhere between the drinks and the music, I felt it hit me—the high of graduating, the memory of Brittany's smile, the echo of that close call behind the wheel. For a few hours, though, none of it mattered. I let the noise swallow everything, living only in the blur of right now.

It wasn't until around midnight that I realized no one I knew was around, and worse, the car we'd arrived in was gone. The club was three or four miles from our hotel. No phone, no ride, no way to reach anyone. My only option was to start walking.

I stuck out my thumb as cars of half-dressed teenagers

screamed past, music blaring, bottles flying out the windows. One group finally pulled over—a beat-up truck with a bed full of New York kids already drunk and yelling over each other. They were headed to a party, but they said they'd give me a ride closer to my hotel. We hit it off fast.

I jumped in the back, where two guys were chugging vodka straight from the handle, and a girl was sitting cross-legged, laughing like a banshee at nothing in particular. We howled at the moon, beat the sides of the truck with our palms, dared each other to yell the dumbest thing at passing cars. One dude ripped off his shirt, stood up while we were rolling, arms outstretched like he was flying. Another lit a joint and passed it around without a care in the world.

But after a while, the driver hollered back, "We're turning off here, bro—not near your hotel." So, they dropped me off on the shoulder, somewhere even farther out. I laughed, waved them off, and started hoofing it again.

About a mile down the road, I heard the thump of bass before I saw the lights—an underground beach bar tucked behind a row of abandoned shacks, word-of-mouth only. The New York crew had mentioned it, so I wandered toward the noise. No ID check, no cover charge—just a pulse of music that pulled you in. Inside, it was packed wall-to-wall with strangers dancing, grinding, climbing on pool tables and countertops, just chaos. Lights flickered, foam rained down in one corner, and the whole place smelled like coconut rum and saltwater.

I spent hours there—dancing with girls I'd never see again, doing shots with random strangers, and watching the crowd as if I were in a fever dream. At some point, a wet t-shirt contest broke out near the back bar, followed by a wildly inappropriate moaning contest that had the whole place howling. Then an ass-shaking contest so outrageous it felt like MTV Spring Break met a hurricane.

When the music finally started to fade and the crowd thinned, I made my way out. My feet were dragging, shirt soaked in a mix of liquor and seawater. It was nearly sunrise when I saw the dull outline of The Chateau in the distance. I stumbled up the beachside path and back into our room, where the others were sprawled out in various states of sleep and hangover.

I dropped down onto a chair, grabbed a can from the cooler, cracked it open, and tossed a few others across the floor.

"Round two?" I said, as the groaning began.

What started as a three-night reservation turned into nine days. My parents were furious when I got home, but it was worth it. I had stories I'll never tell anyone... and some I barely remember myself.

34

TRUE HEARTBREAK

I came home sunburned, sandy, still carrying the laughter and exhaustion of Panama in my bones. I dropped my bag by the door like nothing in the world was heavier than dirty laundry. For the first time in weeks, the air felt calm. Mama was already fussing, her voice sharp but familiar, grounding me back into normal life.

"You could've called," she snapped.

It was the kind of fight I'd expected the whole drive home, and in some strange way, I almost welcomed it. A regular day. A normal homecoming. Until the phone rang.

It was Saxton.

His voice was quiet. Shaken.

"Brittany's in the hospital."

The world tilted.

"She went in a few days ago. It got bad," Saxton continued.

"But she's okay now, right?" I asked, hoping for good news.

Long pause.

"I don't know," he finally said.

I stood there in silence, the beach still in my bones, the

saltwater still in my skin, and suddenly, none of it mattered. The joy, the laughter, the dumb inside jokes—they vanished like breath on a mirror.

I hung up and called Brittany's house. No answer. Called again. Nothing.

I called Saxton back.

"Where is she?" I croaked.

"Erlanger," he said. "In Chattanooga."

"I'm coming."

- - -

The hospital smelled like bleach and grief.

I knew the place. My great-uncle had spent months there after his wreck. Same colorless walls, same endless hallway hum, same gut-deep dread.

We found the floor. Found the room. But the nurse stopped us.

"Only immediate family."

Her brother—quiet kid, same age as me—met us at the doors. His face looked like mine felt, drained, strung out, desperate for something solid to hold onto.

"She couldn't get out of bed that morning," he said. "Vitals crashed. She just... collapsed."

He didn't say much more, just that they were trying. Fighting. Hoping.

Saxton and I sat in the waiting room, pretending we were there for someone else. People walked past, crying, whispering, praying. And there we sat, two boys who suddenly felt small in a world far too big.

I thought about the beach. About Brittany's smile before I left. About how I hadn't even said goodbye, not really.

I thought about her laugh that carried across hallways, the way she tilted her head when she listened, the stubborn strength she wore like armor even when she was tired. I thought about her bright eyes at prom, her quiet courage, the way she had this gift of making me feel lighter just by being in the room.

I thought all these things about her as I sat there, helpless, clinging to scraps of memory like they might hold her here a little longer.

- - -

When they moved her to a regular room, we finally got to see her.

I stepped in and saw her sitting up, facing her mom. When her eyes met mine, they lit up—not bright, not loud, just... warm. Like she'd been waiting for me to show up, and now things could finally settle.

She looked tired, worn thin from the fight, but still her.

Still Brittany.

Still beautiful.

She couldn't talk much. So, I did what I always did—I filled the space with stories. Told her about Panama City. The sand. The chaos. The jokes. What was safe for her mom to hear, anyway. I rambled until her eyes got heavy and she drifted off.

When she woke, her mom handed her a notebook. She scribbled something down and slid it across the blanket to me.

"Can we date when I get out of here?"

God. I laughed, even though my throat was tight. Even though I wanted to cry.

"Of course we can," I said, squeezing her hand. "As soon as you're out, I'm all yours."

I grabbed the pen and wrote back.

"Do you want to be my girlfriend?"

She nodded before she even wrote the answer.

"YES." Big letters. Underlined.

She smiled at me—soft, proud, full of the kind of hope that makes your chest ache.

Before I left, I told her I loved her.

She mouthed it back. Couldn't speak it. But I saw it. Felt it.

And then she scribbled it one more time on the bottom of the page.

"I love you."

- - -

A few days later, I was at a buddy's house, half-planning a fishing trip, when the phone rang. He picked up. Listened. Turned pale.

He looked at me like he didn't want to say what he had to say.

"You need to get to Erlanger," he said. "Now."

No questions. No shoes. No music on the drive. Just me and the storm building in my chest.

- - -

When I walked into that waiting room, I already knew.

Her mom was standing just outside the room, and when she saw me, her face cracked.

She opened her arms like a mother does when she knows a kid's about to break.

"She's still breathing," she said. "But it won't be long. Do you want to see her?"

I nodded.

She let me go in first.

- - -

The room was still. Too still.

Monitors blinked. Machines breathed for her.

She lay there, eyes closed, lips parted just slightly, as if she might whisper something if the air was right.

I walked over and took her hand. It was warm. Still warm. And somehow, that made it worse.

I whispered to her. Told her I was here. Told her I wasn't going anywhere.

Her hair had gotten messy, so her aunt and mom began to wash it gently. I asked if I could stay. They said yes.

I sat there while they brushed through her hair like they had when she was a little girl. Slow, soft strokes. Reverent.

And while they worked, I kept talking to her. Telling her everything I hadn't said. Everything I should have. Everything that could've waited, but now couldn't.

Her note sat on the counter beside her bed.

The note that said, *"I love you."*

It felt like a final breath frozen in ink.

I don't know how long I stayed. Time didn't mean anything anymore.

Eventually, I leaned down, kissed her forehead, and whispered, "You changed me. You saved me. I love you."

Then I let go.

And walked out of the room with her goodbye written in my chest.

- - -

Brittany passed just before midnight.

- - -

I'd lost people before. Grandparents. Distant relatives. Even friends. But this?

This was different.

This was watching light leave the world one flicker at a time.

This was standing in the middle of your own life and realizing the best part of you just slipped away.

And there's no preparing for that.

You don't learn how to say goodbye to someone who gave you the kind of love that made you believe again.

You just carry it.

35

CARRYING THE ACHE

Raye men don't show emotion. We don't cry in public. We bottle it up. Grit our teeth. Power through. At least, that's what I was supposed to do... But not this time.

The morning after the hospital, I walked through my house like a ghost. Everything was louder—footsteps on hardwood, the hum of the fridge, the creak in the floor near the hall closet. My body moved without conscious decision, taking me from one spot to the next.

And then I saw it.

In my house, there was a room Mama turned into her little shrine of family photos. She had hung the prom photos there— junior year and senior year, side by side. Framed. Lit just right by the morning sun bleeding through the window. My eyes gravitated to one spot.

I stood in front of the senior photo. The one from that wonderful night when Brittany laughed at everything and made me feel like maybe—just maybe—I wasn't broken.

I stared into that picture like it might speak. Like it might move. But all it did was stay still. Stay perfect. Stay gone.

My blood moved in my body. I felt it. Cold and slow. Like I wasn't even real.

Then I heard the front door creak open.

My brother walked in. No knock. No warning. Just his heavy boots and quiet presence at the edge of the hallway.

He looked at me. Looked down the hall and saw what I was looking at.

He didn't ask what was wrong.

Didn't smirk or say something sideways like usual.

He just turned his head toward where our mama was and, for maybe the first and only time in our lives, said:

"He's not okay."

That was it.

Three words. No emotion. No hand on the shoulder.

But that wrecked me.

And he knew.

As bad as we hated one another—as cold and distant as our history was—in that single moment, he saw me. The broken pieces. The weight I was drowning in.

He didn't laugh. Didn't scoff. Didn't come closer.

Because there was nothing that could fix what had happened, fix what I felt.

Mama tried to hug me. She came close, tears already forming in her own eyes. She said all the things people say when they're helpless:

"She's in a better place. God has a plan. You'll see her again."

But I couldn't hear it.

Her words just sounded like noise—grief-sweetened gibberish my brain couldn't digest.

I had a funeral to prepare for.

Brittany had touched people. All kinds of people—young and old, teachers and waitresses, classmates and strangers.

And they came.

Hundreds of them.

Not a dry eye in the building.

As I sat there, surrounded by the grief of everyone who'd ever loved her, my mind wandered to every version of Brittany I'd known—the one who smiled through pain, the one who danced at prom, the one who scribbled *"I love you"* in a hospital bed. I could see her lying peacefully in the casket as songs were sung and the preacher spoke words I couldn't hear. The service blurred around me, the voices fading into memory.

When it was my turn to approach the casket for the final goodbye, my hand reached for hers, and I felt the coldness of what used to be a warm soul. My mind replayed the time we'd flirtatiously passed each other in the school hallway on a "bathroom" break, our hands brushing together. I remember the tears, the ache in my chest—but not the sound of my own voice, though I know I was saying *"no"* as they gently pulled me away.

People stood shoulder to shoulder in that church, some spilling out into the halls, all of them holding back the same scream I had living under my ribs.

Her mom knew.

She hugged me that first night during visitation, held on like I was the last warm thing in the world. She whispered in my ear, voice cracked but strong.

"Thank you," she told me. "You gave her prom. You gave her something else to think about besides cancer. She smiled after you left. She showed me the letter. I knew."

She knew.

Brittany's mom had seen the light in her daughter's face before it faded forever.

And there I was, trying to hold it together, telling myself, "Stop crying. Stop breaking down. *She* wouldn't want this."

But I couldn't.

Not this time.

I'd dealt with years of loss—people taken by death or by their own damn choices, and then had to stand there as the one with the purest soul I'd ever known was being lowered into the ground.

And I had to watch.

I had to watch the casket close.

Had to watch it lower, slow and smooth, like they were afraid to wake her.

Had to watch the dirt get shoveled on top, like it didn't weigh more than the world itself.

It was a thousand knives in my lungs.

And no matter how much you prepare, how strong you pretend to be, you can't breathe through that.

I visited her grave often that summer.

Sometimes I brought flowers. Sometimes I brought silence. Sometimes I just sat there and hoped the wind might bring Brittany's voice back to me.

Six, seven years later, I still went.

The pain doesn't leave. It just changes shape. I was forever changed.

That summer?

I was distant. Cold. Lost in a way that didn't show on the outside but gutted me inside. I walked through days like they were dreams I couldn't wake from.

She was gone.

And with her went whatever plans that might've been.

The map was gone.

And all I had left was the unbearable ache.

36

UNDECIDED PATHS

Despite the pain I carried, I had to do what I learned to do best—make fun of myself, play the jokester, make people laugh, hide my insecurities, and fight the war on the inside. But for many months, I no longer knew what I was fighting for.

Some people think that when you're a certain age, you're grown. You make "grown" decisions, and you know the way. In reality, you don't—no matter if you're sixteen, nineteen, twenty-five, or thirty. Because as I write this today, I'm still learning each day.

That summer, after high school and the funeral, was a blur. The hurt, the pain, the blame—not just from her, but from all the losses beforehand—had been sitting on my chest for years. Then that last petal lay down, and it snapped everything.

I had navigated through thirteen years of school. I was still young, but my body, my heart, and my mind felt double my age. Your soul grows old when you're constantly fighting—fighting your own reflection, your doubts, the deaths, the goodbyes. I had lived through experiences some don't taste until their late twenties, and I'd already felt the full weight of them five to eight years earlier.

One of the only things that saved me—I believe—was the fact that Rayes are strong. My dad taught me that. Not with words, but with presence. With that head of his lifted high at the end of the table. Now, I understand that back then, he didn't have all the answers either. But he provided. He endured. He carried on. So, as bad as it hurt some days that summer, I knew I had to lift my head, too, even if just barely, and keep grinding toward some kind of future.

The future... oh boy. Who knew? I didn't. But I knew it didn't look like staying home, leeching off aging parents, barely scraping by, risking the fall into what had swallowed up too many Rayes before me. I could feel the town changing, too. Crystal meth—this slow-moving, silent killer—had crept out of the shadows. It didn't care who you were. Rich, poor. Athlete, dropout. Alive, dying. Just like other towns in the South, we had our fair share of weed, cocaine, and I'd even seen heroin and crack now and then. But meth... meth was different. It used to belong to the run-down neighborhoods. Then it didn't.

It wasn't just strangers losing themselves to meth either. I had cousins, acquaintances, and classmates that started using, and I watched their lives crumble in slow motion. You think you'll be able to spot the line between "a little fun" and "too far," but with meth, there's no line. It just eats everything. I never crossed that line. I still had other things to focus on.

It was time to go to junior college. I said I would. I had a free ride to do so. What was I going to do? No idea.

No Raye had ever walked on any kind of college campus before, from small to large. And that summer, I didn't prepare.

I didn't look into majors, schedules, dorms, or anything else. I just knew I had to show up one day to meet someone about getting into classes. So, I did, and the very first sign I wasn't ready came within three minutes.

"What degree will you be pursuing?" the advisor questioned.

Wait. What?

"What do you mean?" I asked.

"What degree do you hope to obtain when you're done?" she said, rattling off options so fast my mind tapped out around the fifth one.

What degree? Hell, I was barely even there at that moment. I chose "Undecided," and that was more honest than anyone could've imagined.

Some kids picked that because they couldn't decide between being a general elementary teacher or a college math professor. Some weren't sure if they'd be engineers or computer scientists, doctors or nurse practitioners.

Me? Undecided meant I was damn lucky to even be here. I had no blueprint, no clue what I was supposed to be doing. So, I got slotted into general education classes. The ones everybody takes, no matter what they're aiming for.

What they don't tell you is: Nobody's going to make you do anything. If you didn't go to class? Oh well. No one called home. No notes. No check-ins. The professor didn't care if he had a hundred students or ten. If you failed, you failed. If your GPA dropped too low, you lost your scholarship and paid out of pocket if you even stuck around.

The best thing for me back then? College was only about a 15-20 minute drive from home. Sometimes I'd head to work after class, so I left the house each morning. That helped. Just leaving the house. Just having somewhere to be. It kept me afloat.

Even then, I skipped math on some days to play Rook in the student lounge. That first fall semester, I barely socialized. I'd spot a few familiar faces from Eagle High or rival schools, boys I once played against or watched on Friday nights, or shot the breeze with at parties. Hell, I even buried the hatchet with two of the guys from the moonshine and football fight.

Though not because I was mature.

It was mostly because I didn't have the energy to care anymore.

They probably thought I'd grown up or gotten over it. Truth was, if they'd wanted to fight again, I probably would've said, "Okay," and kept walking. But instead, they apologized. They asked for forgiveness. And I just said, "Okay," and kept walking.

One thing I did have to do, because of the scholarship, was take theater classes. So, every Monday, Wednesday, and Friday, around 1:00 p.m., I showed up at the theater.

At first, I worked behind the scenes—building sets, painting, and cleaning up tools for the upcoming play. But as weeks passed, something shifted. I watched the students, as well as the adults, rehearse their lines. I saw them become someone else. They weren't just acting—they were escaping.

And it wasn't about being seen. That's what most people don't get.

For me, it wasn't about people watching me under a spotlight. It was about vanishing. Stepping into a skin that wasn't mine. Leaving behind the weight of my name, my losses, my past—even if just for a few hours. It was freedom in costume.

This was freedom I received thanks to Mr. Webb—the man who believed in me enough to offer me the scholarship. He gave me a chance to experience that freedom. Standing in that theater, watching that world unfold, I started to believe in him, too.

He'd walk through the stage of half-finished sets with that quiet patience teachers don't get paid enough for. Sometimes, he'd stop beside me and ask about the build—not about my life, just the work. But somehow, those small conversations kept me steady. He had a way of making you feel capable without ever saying the words. I didn't realize it then, but he was teaching me more than theater. He was teaching me how to show up and believe again.

He became the mentor I never knew I needed—quiet, present, honest. He didn't try to fix me or pry into the hurt I carried. He just gave me something to do, something to build, and eventually, a space to breathe. For the first time in a long time, that felt like enough to keep me going.

But like all things that save you, I didn't know how fragile that balance really was.

37

STORMS AND SHADOWS

That Christmas break felt different than all the ones before. In high school, we'd always come back to the same hallways, same classrooms, swapping stories about presents, trips, who hooked up, who broke up. But not this time.

This time, some folks didn't come back at all.

The ones who did come back had their own circles, their own timelines, their own lives. They weren't interested in the past—they were trying to outrun it, just like I was.

So, for the first time, I spent that whole break mostly at home or at work. Saxton was out with his crew, finishing his senior year with bonfires and backroads. I just floated. Back home, people expected you to bring back something. A plan. A dream. A damn purpose. But all I had were shrugs and a lump in my throat I couldn't swallow.

Principal John apparently made a speech to start the next school year at Eagle High, telling the whole school that I was no longer among them. Said it like a warning. Like an example. Maybe he meant well, maybe he didn't—but hearing about it later felt like confirmation of what I already knew: I'd become a story people told, not a person they asked about. Another name lost in the halls I used to walk.

The spring semester started with less confusion and more weight. I figured I might as well make myself useful. The next production was *Fiddler on the Roof*, and even though I'd never sung on stage—hell, barely sang outside my truck—I signed up anyway for tryouts.

Classes were smoother, too. I'd shoved my next math class into next year's problem pile. Most days, I made it. Some days, I didn't.

Then there was that storm.

It was a Southern spring kind of storm, with thunder that felt personal. The kind that doesn't just roll in. It stalks you.

I didn't mean to go to Brittany's grave that day. Didn't plan it. Was just driving. Rain was just starting, clouds folding in on themselves.

Then "Free Bird" came on the radio.

I hadn't heard it in months, and somehow it felt like something bigger than music. As if someone was trying to say something. I reached over and turned it up, letting it fill the cab.

Before I knew it, I was pulling onto the gravel road and following that old dirt road for miles. Not a city or church cemetery, but more like some family land where loved ones were placed.

The pines leaned over like they were holding their breath. Rain tapped the windshield, steady at first, like a warning knock on the door.

I saw her name before I got out. *Brittany.* The stone was

clean. Too clean. Someone had been by.

There were fresh flowers.

A note, sealed in a plastic bag. Weighed down by a rock.

And a shape off in the distance.

I swear there was someone standing there. Not moving. Not doing anything. Just... there.

Slim. Still. Wearing what looked like a coat or dress—could've been the light, could've been the rain. I blinked. Looked again.

The figure? Gone.

I stepped out anyway.

Didn't speak. Didn't cry. Just stood there, letting the rain soak into my bones. Listening to the ending solo of "Free Bird" bleed out through my open truck door.

As I stepped out, my eyes caught sight of the shotgun in the backseat. Dad's old 20 gauge. I'd picked it up from Dad's cabinet a few weeks earlier, thinking I might take it hunting with a buddy, but I never did. It had just been riding around ever since—quiet, heavy, forgotten until that day.

Sat in the backsteat wrapped in an old towel. Grandpa's.

Not loaded. Not yet.

I left it there, however, with its presence lingering at the edges of my mind.

I didn't want to feel like I was crazy. But that figure... it rattled me. Felt like maybe Brittany hadn't been ready to leave yet. Maybe I wasn't either.

After a while, I got back in the truck. Drove east, toward Grandpa's plot, with the sky going black and angry above the tree line.

The road narrowed as I got closer. That shotgun rattled in

the back with every bump.

Didn't matter. I wasn't changing my mind—I just didn't know what my mind was yet.

The cemetery was empty. Except for one old pickup parked off to the side, dusted in pine straw like it had been forgotten. Felt right somehow.

I pulled in, sat for a minute, engine humming, heater on low. Then I stepped out.

Rain hit hard now. Sheets of it. No room to think, just move. Boots sank in the mud. Wind cut through me.

I found Grandpa's marker. Simple. Military tag rusting into the ground. I dropped to my knees.

"I don't know what I'm doing," I whispered. "I'm tired."

Then thunder hit—close. Violent. Like God slamming a fist on the table.

Suddenly, there were headlights.

Headlights from another truck, crawling into the lot.

The door creaked open. A figure stepped out.

Brittany's brother.

"What the hell you doin' out here, man?" he called, squinting through the storm.

I stood up, dripping, voice rough as I said, "Could ask you the same."

"Had a feeling," he said. "Gut told me to take the long way home. Saw your truck. Had to stop."

I didn't say anything. Didn't tell him about the shotgun. Or the figure. Or the song.

He gestured toward his truck. "You're soaked. Come on."

We lumbered our way to his truck, climbing inside. We sat in silence, heat blasting, both of us steaming. The storm raged on outside.

We didn't talk about Brittany. We didn't talk about what I saw or thought I saw.

We talked about music. About loneliness. About how much pretending it takes just to make it through a day.

After a while, I said I should head out. He didn't stop me.

"You good?" he asked.

I didn't lie.

"I don't know."

And that was enough.

I didn't touch the gun that night. Didn't tell my parents. Didn't sleep much either.

I still don't know if that talk saved me or if it was something else. But either way, it got me through the night, and that was all I needed. I made it to the next day.

And somewhere down the line—months, maybe years later—I told a stranger about that night.

I got help.

But I still remember that rain. Still hear "Free Bird" playing. Still feel the weight of that gun.

And sometimes, when it's quiet, I still wonder—

Who was watching me in those woods?

38
A NEW CHANCE

Saxton decided to take the scholarship offer to Auburn University, where they also had a degree he was genuinely interested in. It made sense—he had direction, a path, something to chase. Me? I was still trudging along in junior college. Just wrapped up a run in Fiddler on the Roof, where I was a secondary character in a few scenes and helped backstage on the crew. It kept my mind busy and gave me a reason to be around other college-minded folks, which helped. I'd finally found a rhythm with school, pulling A's and B's, keeping my GPA in decent shape. But I knew, once summer was over, the questions would start again.

What now? Where next?

I'd gone on a few double dates, mostly with Brent and whatever girlfriend he was trying to keep that week. But truth be told, I wasn't really interested. Somewhere along the way, I'd started believing that whenever I got close to someone— really close—they either moved away, lost interest, or died. The pattern was too real to ignore, and it kept me guarded.

Got a job at the plant in town. The plant was a rug maker.

The plant wasn't bad work, but it was the kind that ate at you slowly. The smell of new rugs mixed with forklift propane clung to your clothes, and the hum of the machines never left your ears, even after you clocked out. Most of the men there had the same look in their eyes—tired, beaten, waiting for the next weekend to forget the one before. I respected them, but I knew if I stayed, that look would find me too. The place was known to hold the ones who didn't leave for the better.

That was when it started to really settle in: Sand Mountain wasn't going to be home forever. It couldn't be.

The Valley was fading—businesses leaving, jobs drying up, and the talk of turning it into a retirement community near the river seemed more real by the day. The mountain? Same as always. A few family-run shops, gas stations, Dollar Generals, and a whole lot of ghosts from the past. The circle I once had was either off chasing trades, wrapped in school, or slipping under the weight of addiction. I looked around and saw nothing but echoes of better days, shadows of laughter that used to ring through the woods and down the gravel roads.

That summer, I picked up a role in a small-town production. Played a mute, which felt oddly fitting. Theater had become my temporary escape. A stage where I could be someone else, even if just for a little while. But deep down, I knew it wasn't my future. I wasn't that good, and I couldn't afford to chase a dream that didn't want me back. The scholarship I had was only good for two more semesters, and my family didn't have a dime to throw toward tuition. My ACT score from high school wasn't worth bragging about, and even with my GPA hovering around 2.8 to 3.0, my chances of a new scholarship were slim.

Then came the night that changed everything.

It was the start of the fall semester, 2003. I was home for supper on a random weekday night, just like old times. Dad sat in his usual spot at the head of the table, and Mama sat across from me. We started passing dishes, the clatter of forks and plates filling the kitchen. I'd barely gotten in my first bite when Dad spoke.

"Son, I think it's time you fully commit to the plant you're at. They can move you to first shift. It's good money, and with a few years of hard work, you could move up to team lead, supervisor, maybe. You've done good, son. Finished high school, earned that scholarship, made it two years. We're proud."

His words sank into me like cold water. Because he was right. He couldn't afford to send me off somewhere else, and the plant was steady work. Safe. But part of me crumbled inside. I nodded, trying to smile, but all I could think was: *'I can't stay here. I'll rot if I do.'*

Still, I heard him out, not wanting to interrupt.

"See if they can work it into a two-year degree," Dad said. "If not, use what you've got on your résumé. It means something."

He meant well. And hearing him say he was proud—it hit different. But the truth? I was scared. Because I didn't know how to leave. But I just knew I had to.

The next morning, I drove to college earlier than usual. I didn't have class till later, but I needed to talk to someone— anyone—about where the hell I was headed. I went straight to the advisor's office, hoping maybe there was some last-minute miracle they could pull out of a drawer. Maybe some option I hadn't considered. Maybe some path I could slide into with the remaining scholarship time I had left.

But as I feared, my lack of direction had caught up with me. The advisor flipped through my file, nodded politely, and explained that most of what I'd taken was just general ed. The same classes nearly every freshman and sophomore end up with. Useful, sure. But not for much. Not for a plant résumé. Not for the dream I didn't know how to name.

"You could always transfer," she said. "Almost every four-year university will accept these courses."

I half-laughed, telling her, "Wish I could transfer 'em to my plant job in the Valley. Maybe knock a couple of years off my wait for a raise."

She caught the joke—or maybe the bitterness hiding under it, and gave a soft smile. I shrugged.

"I'm the one-eyed Raye," I said with a grin that didn't reach my eyes. "Maybe this is as far as I was ever supposed to come."

Then something strange happened.

She reached across the desk and gently grabbed my arm. Her face had shifted, suddenly serious.

"What did you just say?"

I looked at her, confused. "Uh... that maybe this is as far as I was ever supposed to come?"

"No, before that," she said, holding eye contact.

I hesitated. "One-eyed Raye?"

She let go of my arm and started digging through her desk drawers like she was looking for something she hadn't touched in years. Papers rustled. Folders flapped. Then suddenly she lit up like she'd found buried treasure.

"I knew I still had it," she said. "Claxton, I think you might have a chance here."

She handed me a yellow sticky note with a name and a

number scribbled on it.

"Call this guy, his name's Brian. Tell him I told you to reach out. And tell him about your eye."

I was even more confused, looking from her to the sticky note.

"You want me to call a stranger and tell him I was born blind in my left eye?"

She smiled like I was being thick.

"Yes. Because the state has funding for students with qualifying disabilities. They cover schooling—fully, in some cases."

"Disability?" I said, like the word tasted bad. "I ain't disabled. I can do anything any other kid can do. I'm fine."

She didn't argue. Just looked at me, calm and sure.

"I'm not saying you're not capable," she explained. "I'm saying maybe you've had to do more than most just to be seen as average. That counts. And you owe it to yourself to make that call. Even if it goes nowhere. Even if it's just one more dead end. *Try.*"

I folded the sticky note and stuck it in my pocket, not knowing if it was real hope or just another wild lead. But for the first time in a long time, the road ahead didn't feel so narrow. Maybe this was it—the break I'd been too stubborn to see. Maybe, just maybe, it was my new chance.

39

GAME DAY REALIZATION

I didn't call the number immediately. Didn't even think about it, really. Not because I forgot, but because I figured there was no point. My chances were hopeless, and I wasn't about to start calling myself disabled. That word felt heavy, like defeat. And I wasn't defeated. Not yet.

It was mid-September, halfway through my sophomore fall semester at the junior college. I was doing well enough— classes weren't killing me—but the constant grind was wearing on me. Late nights at the plant, early mornings in classrooms. I was tired more than I wasn't. Sleep was a luxury. Hope, even more so.

Then Saxton called one morning and invited me down to Auburn for the weekend. I checked my schedule, made sure I was off work, and told my folks I'd be gone for a couple of days. My dad made a few Auburn jokes, puzzled as to why I'd go visit there at all. Said I better not tell too many people I was heading that way. I just smiled, threw some clothes in the car, and hit the road. I'd never looked at a map to see where Auburn actually was. I just knew it was south. So, I dropped down I-59 off the mountain, figuring I'd sort it out by the time I hit Birmingham. Bad move. That route added at least an extra hour, probably more. But after a few gas station stops, a couple of wrong turns, and plenty of map-checking, I made it. Auburn.

Saxton lived in a trailer park right off Wire Road. The place had over 500 trailers, and every single one of them seemed to be packed with students. I pulled in and was instantly floored—kids everywhere, music thumping from yards, beer cans on porches, laughter spilling out into the street. It was like spring break in Panama City, except this wasn't the beach. This was college life.

And it was a game day weekend.

Saxton met me outside and laughed when I told him I thought the traffic coming in was bad. He said I hadn't seen anything yet. He drove me around first, showed me the campus, the stadium, and Toomer's Corner. Then we visited a few folks from back home—other Sand Mountain kids who had made it to Auburn. A few older Eagle High grads, some familiar faces from rival schools. Everyone was planning to meet at Saxton's trailer later for drinks before heading out.

It felt like a different world.

That afternoon, we drank beers, played games, and watched TV. No parents. No rules. Freedom. I stepped out for a smoke and met two random guys in their yard. They raised their beers to me and shouted, "War Eagle!" like I'd been part of their crew for years.

Later, we piled into a guy named Daniel's truck and headed to a Mexican joint near the bar strip. I still had my fake ID in my wallet, so I threw back a couple of margaritas with my Speedy Gonzales #1 meal and stared, probably too long, at the unreal number of beautiful college girls in that place. They didn't leave much to the imagination.

Then it was off to The Highlands—a bar that, on this Friday night before a home game, was slammed. Shoulder-to-shoulder. Every walk of life. Every color, background, story. But all of them were young, loud, and alive. The energy was like lightning.

I was halfway through a mixed drink when I heard it.

"Well damn, is that ole 20/20 himself in Auburn?"

I turned, and sure enough, more high school buddies were there. "20/20" had been a nickname tossed at me a few times in school—joking about my eye—but never enough to stick. That would change in the years to come. That night, though, it made me laugh.

We drank, laughed, yelled over the music, and soaked up every drop of that wild night. By the time we stumbled back to the trailer park, the sun was starting to rise. But the party didn't stop. It just changed shapes. Saxton's trailer buzzed with life.

And then came game day.

The whole town turned orange and blue. Tailgates sprang up like mushrooms. Beer pong on every patch of grass. Music, food, yelling, hugs from strangers. I even played a game of HORSE with a cop while sipping a beer. This wasn't Sand Mountain. Not even close.

And as I stood there in that sea of energy and opportunity, I thought: *'How do I get down here?'*

That was when I remembered the sticky note.

If I wanted this—this life, this shot, this escape—I had to make the call. The number was still sitting in my wallet. Just waiting. Like maybe it had been this whole time.

40
THE LAST STRAW

I knew I needed to start making a real plan for my life. You'd think heading to Auburn to be with friends and chase that degree would be the top priority—but it wasn't that simple. I still had to finish up junior college. Pass that damn math class. Work. Save.

And then there was Becky.

That little sandy-blonde "friend" situation had crept up on me when I wasn't paying attention. We met in theater. What started as a friendly face became something more, even though I tried to fight it. Why? Because I didn't want it. I'd lost enough already. But somewhere along the way, I started to question if I wanted to leave her behind. Could I leave her behind? Should I?

I thought, *'Maybe I could wait a year. Maybe we could go together.'*

We started hanging out more. First in groups. Then just us. It was clear from the start that Becky was an 18-year-old wild child. She was a firecracker with a body and voice that could bring a man to his knees, and she damn well knew it. She was popular. Dangerous. Crazy. Everything I didn't want—yet everything I kept coming back to, like a blind mouse chasing cheese.

Becky wasn't from my world. While I was partying in backfields and wooded clearings, she was sneaking into clubs in Chattanooga, dating older guys, and winning moaning contests at the biggest clubs in Tennessee. Yeah, you heard that right. Moaning contests. Theater brought her in—her looks and her voice got her on stage, but her history made her unforgettable.

Her ex? Five years older, three times my size. So, it begged the question: Why the hell was she hanging out with me?

I didn't know. I didn't care. Not at first. But eventually... I did.

That last semester of junior college for me was her first. Her being at my side made every guy in the student hall stare and wonder what the hell was going on. But I kept her laughing, and maybe that was the only thing keeping her there.

The nudges under the table during Rook games, the stolen kisses in the dark corners of the theater, the backseat make-out sessions—they started to stack up. I found myself second-guessing that transfer application. My college advisor was pushing me in one direction, but Becky was pulling me in another.

I told myself it could be different with Becky. Maybe she'd see the parts of me no one else had bothered to look at. Maybe love didn't have to be clean or patient—maybe it could just be loud enough to drown out the past. It sounds foolish now, but when you're broken, even the wrong kind of attention feels like salvation. I wasn't thinking about the future. Just about Becky. When she flirted with other guys and gave me that wicked grin while doing it, it started to burn. Nights when she didn't show up or call? That shit stuck with me, made me wonder what I was even doing. Why couldn't I shake the hold she had on me?

Maybe I kept her around because she made me feel something again. After Brittany, I'd gone numb—no highs, no lows, just noise. But Becky? She was chaos and color. She reminded me what it was like to be wanted, even if it was all smoke. I told myself it wasn't serious, but deep down, I think I just needed proof I could still feel anything at all.

It started to feel like maybe I shouldn't leave. I had a decent thing going here—steady work, a girl, some attention. Why risk it all for a town my family hated and a dream that might never come true?

I had graduated high school. That alone made my folks proud. I'd done two years at junior college and had a decent job at the plant. Maybe this was enough. Maybe Becky was part of that equation.

Until the last straw broke.

Remember years ago when my brother blackmailed me and I helped convince my parents he needed his own place? Yeah. I hadn't really seen him since Brittany's death. I was fine with that.

But he wasn't done with me.

It was a Friday night. I had the night off from the plant, which was rare. I had planned to visit Saxton in Auburn, but at the last minute, I bailed. Decided I'd surprise Becky instead. Maybe take her out. Maybe say what I hadn't yet. I even debated flowers—but nah, Becky was too cool for that cheesy shit.

I drove to Becky's place. She wasn't home.

Said she would be. Said she was chillin' with her sisters.

Told me to have fun in Auburn.

I called. *No answer.* Texted. *Nothing.*

Fine. Maybe she was out. No big deal, I told myself.

Then Plug texted: "Party at Dave's."

Dave's place was notorious. Used to be legendary. Lately, more of a haven for the hard stuff—coke, pills. Not my scene. But I didn't want to go home either.

I knew something was off the moment I saw that damn Toyota long bed parked like a rusted-out trophy at the edge of the yard. That stick-shift junker had no business being at a party like this anymore—unless it was dragging trouble in behind it. Plug caught my expression before I even opened my mouth.

"Clax... calm down, man. I'm sure he's off somewhere, away from the crowd. Just drink a beer, chill."

I nodded, pretending to listen, but every muscle in me was already tightening.

The house was alive. Music pounding out of every window, the porch strung with Christmas lights that cast everybody in a hazy glow. Beer bottles clinked, people laughed, and the smell of weed, sweat, and spilled liquor turned the summer air thick. It was a classic throwback party—one of those barnburners you hear about for months after—but I wasn't here to party anymore.

Then I saw him.

Standing on the porch, leaning with that smugness that only he could pull off, was my brother. Metal jaw. Crooked grin. Still breathing somehow.

He looked down at me like he'd been waiting for this moment his whole damn life.

Then... there she was.

Becky.

Hair tossed over one shoulder, arms around his waist like she was molded there, smiling like the devil herself. He twirled her to the music—Pearl Jam's "Better Man"—and she giggled as he leaned in. Their lips touched. Tongues tangled. Her eyes peeked open just long enough to find mine in the crowd.

That was the moment something snapped.

It didn't feel like anger. It felt like gravity. Like the earth tilted and all of it was pulling me up that hill, through the people, over the railing, toward him. I dropped the bottle in my hand. Didn't even hear it shatter. Didn't feel the thorns rip into my shins as I barreled through the hedges.

"Can't find a better man..." The music crooned.

I leapt—one hand on the porch rail, the other clenched so tight my knuckles cracked.

I hit my brother square in the chest, a full-bodied tackle that sent us both flying through the porch furniture like wreckage in a storm. Wood split, a table flipped, people screamed, and suddenly all the music in the background was drowned out by one chant.

"FIGHT! FIGHT! FIGHT!"

He scrambled up first, blood already trickling from his lip. I charged again. Swing. Miss. He caught me in the ribs with a knee. I buckled but didn't go down. I got one clean punch to the side of his head—metal jaw or not, he staggered. I felt it. People backed away, clearing a circle. Plug was yelling something behind me, but I was already in a red haze.

"Sweet Child O' Mine" was blasting now. Like the soundtrack to the worst damn movie of my life. Guitars screaming while fists flew. He got in closer, more methodical. Military. Precise. I fought like an animal. One of my swings caught him in the neck—he reeled, but then came back with a right hook that rattled something loose in my skull. Blood flooded my mouth. My knees dipped. He grabbed my shirt collar and threw me back-first into a wooden post that cracked on impact. Everything around me started to blur, but I still pushed off the ground and came again.

I don't know how long we fought. Time slowed, stretched out. It was like every punch was a memory—we were brawling over every missed birthday, every insult, every manipulative threat he'd ever thrown at me. Every stolen moment.

I landed one more solid shot. His head snapped. For a second, I thought I had him.

But then he caught me right in the mouth, and everything blurred.

I fell to my knees, one hand bracing against the porch floor. I tried to stand—blood dripping from my lip, rage pulsing in my ears—but I looked up, and there she was again.

Becky.

Smiling.

Smiling.

She tucked her body against his like nothing had happened. Like I was some entertainment on a Saturday night, not the guy who thought maybe—just maybe—he could build a life with her.

But in that moment, all those thoughts faded to the background as I blurredly stared at them.

My brother wrapped his arms around her like a prize. Like I had been nothing but a bridge to get to her.

I collapsed forward, arms giving out.

Not because he beat me.

But because I saw it then, clearer than ever.

Becky was never mine.

She never intended to be.

Plug and two others helped me off the porch, all quiet except for a few drunken chants trailing off and Axl Rose wailing into the sky. As I stumbled through the crowd, faces were turned away, and nobody was cheering anymore. Just whispers and wide eyes. I knew I was done here.

Done with her.

Done with him.

Done with this town.

That Monday morning, I pulled out the sticky note and called the number the advisor gave me.

It wasn't about running anymore. It was about finally choosing me—choosing to build something instead of bleed for it. The ringtone sounded like freedom, and I knew this time, I wasn't looking back.

41

THE WAR I STARTED BY LEAVING

Fighting ran in the Raye bloodline. Always had. My uncles, my grandpa, my dad—they'd all brawled through life with fists, stubbornness, and pride. But Rayes didn't fight Rayes. That was the code. Unspoken, passed down like hand-me-down boots or the smell of motor oil on a Sunday shirt. Family was sacred. Blood above all.

So, when my brother and I beat the hell out of each other on that porch, something deeper cracked open. Not just bones or pride. It felt like betrayal. Like I'd crossed a line that Rayes weren't supposed to cross—another line, after a long list of others.

I'd always been different.

Always.

And I wasn't done disappointing folks just yet.

Because not long after the fight, I made the announcement that would rip through our family like a lightning bolt on a dry pine.

I'd been accepted to Auburn University. To most people, it was a dream come true. To us? It was damn near treason.

Sure, my mama and dad were proud. Hell, I know they were. But I also saw it in my old man's eyes—the way he stared off longer, quieter. The way his jaw set like stone every time someone brought it up. He supported me, but it wasn't easy for him. I get it now.

For a Sand Mountain family baptized in crimson and houndstooth, I might as well have burned the Bible.

One of my uncles, my mama's own blood, never spoke another word to me after I left. Not one. He just… disappeared. Never said goodbye. Never said he was disappointed. He just cut me off like I was a cancer. That's the thing about the Crimson Tide—sometimes it ran thicker than family.

But I had an ace from above, something I never saw coming.

Turns out, my bad eye had finally done something good. Between the scarred retina and the vision so poor it made me half-blind on paper, I qualified for a special type of state financial aid. If I could maintain a certain GPA, the state would pay for my entire tuition.

A miracle. A lifeline.

And it came just in time.

I finished junior college and theater that May, riding high, except for one little thing—I had to drop math again or risk failing it completely. I told myself I'd figure it out in Auburn. It was just numbers, right?

I was accepted for the summer of 2004—easier than fall—and I didn't hesitate. After the fights, betrayals, and years of barely hanging on in Sand Mountain, I was ready to disappear. Only my parents told me goodbye. My mama cried and tried to hide her worry behind hugs and packed snacks, like holding on tight or slipping notes in my bag could somehow keep me safe.

My dad stayed strong but quiet. I think they both knew I wasn't coming back. Not really. Not to stay.

I moved into a trailer park with Saxton. Kelly, his sister, stayed with us on and off, dating one of our old friends from high school who had also made it to Auburn. And just like that, I was gone.

Gone from everything I knew.

Gone from everyone who knew me.

I was a mountain boy dropped into a city of 40,000 students, more pavement than pasture, more bars than barns.

I had three classes that summer. On day one, I stepped into an auditorium with over 500 students—most of them smarter, richer, and way more confident. The professor didn't even look at us. Just tossed the syllabus on a screen and started talking.

Nobody cared if I was there. Hell, nobody even knew I was there.

I learned quick that if I had class at 8:00 a.m., I needed to leave the trailer by 6:45 a.m. or earlier just to park, hike across campus, and find the right room. If my next class was across campus, I'd be lucky to make it at all. Auburn might as well have been New York City to me.

But I adjusted in my own way.

I partied.

Lord, I partied.

Partying wasn't about fun this time, not really. It was about forgetting. For the first time in my life, I didn't have anyone expecting anything from me, and that kind of freedom felt like falling. Every drink, every laugh, every blurry night helped me drown out the fear that I wasn't supposed to be here in the first place. We traded six-packs for kegs, Friday nights for seven-day benders. We threw parties in trailers, apartments, frat houses, and the damn national forest. I'd wake up with someone else's couch pillow under my head, half a Whopper in my hand, and the lingering regret of an accounting quiz I never made it to.

I arrived in Auburn weighing a lean 180 pounds at 6'3". By the summer of 2005, I tipped the scale at 280. Stress, booze, late-night Krystals, and freedom packed it on like insulation.

I only came home once that whole first year, and that was only for Christmas.

My parents visited a few times. Checked in. Brought groceries. Smiled, though I could see the worry behind their eyes.

Saxton and I held it down in the trailer. Kelly was around, but she was more of a ghost than a roommate. The trailer was barely two bedrooms, thin walls, and air-conditioning that worked only when it felt like it. But it was ours. No parents, no curfew, no rules. At night, when the noise died down and Saxton was passed out, I'd lay there listening to trains roll through town and wonder if this was what growing up was supposed to feel like—lonely, loud, and somehow alive all at once.

One of my first classes was Accounting 1. I picked business logistics as my major because it sounded cool during advising, and I figured it matched up with what I was already good at— figuring things out under pressure.

I studied for my first test harder than I had ever studied in my life. Flashcards. Late nights. Highlighters everywhere. I walked into that test buzzing with confidence. Walked out thinking I'd earned at least a solid B.

That Monday, I got my grade.

D-minus.

The blood drained from my body. I'd worked harder than ever before... and it wasn't enough. Not even close. And that aid? That gift from the state? It could vanish just like that if I didn't hold my GPA.

That should've been the wake-up call. The slap across the face that got me back in line.

But no.

Instead, I drank more.

Because Fall 2004 was coming. My first football season as an Auburn Tiger. I'd heard stories. Tailgates that never ended. Students rolling Toomer's Oaks after every win. The roar of 87,000 fans in Jordan-Hare. I needed to feel like I belonged to something again.

I finished that summer with a 2.5 GPA—barely hanging on.

But I was still there.

Still fighting, just not the Raye way.

Not with fists.

But with stubbornness.

With survival.

42

AUBURN'S WILD RIDE

Boy, I thought summer in my new environment was wild—until I met the fall semester at Auburn University. Holy shit, the people. The whole damn city swelled like it was going to pop wide open. You couldn't even walk into Walmart during move-in week.

And we still had a few weeks before football season even started.

That weekend before classes kicked off? Probably the biggest party weekend I'd ever experienced in my life. Everywhere you went, there were keg parties, house parties, trailer park blowouts, packed bars.

And the ladies? Oh my... they were everywhere. Some of them looked like they'd just been let out of a cage for the first time in their lives. I dated a little, if you could call it that. Mostly, I was chasing distraction, not connection. I didn't trust it yet. Maybe I didn't trust myself either.

After Brittany and then the downfall of Becky, I was done with anything remotely looking like connection. Honestly, that senior year prom photo of Brittany never left my little hole of a room at the trailer. The bruises from my fight with my brother faded, but the memory of how Becky played me hadn't. So, I wasn't looking for anything serious and mostly kept myself busy.

I had five classes that fall. Two were easy electives I picked just to boost my GPA: Organic Gardening and Bowling. Yep, gardening and bowling. We were outside digging around in the dirt, learning to grow plants the organic way... and twice a week, I was at the lanes rolling strikes and spares. Easy credits.

But those other three classes? The hardest I'd ever taken. World Literature I nearly cracked my brain open trying to make sense of Homer's Odyssey.

Then came September 4th—the first Auburn football game of the season. It was a wild, fun day, but nothing compared to the week leading up to the LSU game.

Hurricane Ivan tore through Gulf Shores and came up through Auburn just days before kickoff. We responded the only way we knew how—by having hurricane parties and drinking through the worry that the game might get canceled. But by Friday, it had cleared out, and Saturday morning greeted us with a perfect orange and blue sky. We were 2–0 and ready to find out if this team could handle LSU.

Tailgating for a major SEC rival? Nothing like it. Hundreds of thousands of people flooded Auburn. Our Northeast Alabama crew had our usual on-campus tailgating spot locked down. And suddenly, all that old high school rival crap? It didn't matter anymore. We stood together for our part of the state—unified in Auburn orange and blue.

Tailgating was an all-day, all-night event—high-fiving cops as you threw horseshoes, drinking, cooking, watching TVs hooked up to generators, music blaring, and trash-talking LSU fans as they walked by. You either found a tree to piss behind or got lucky enough to stumble into a bathroom. Nobody cared—as long as you weren't causing real trouble, the cops left you be.

Fights broke out, chants echoed down the road, and school pride buzzed in the air. When we stepped into Jordan-Hare that day, it was electric. #5 LSU vs #14 Auburn. Sold out. 87,000 fans. Everyone in the student section was on their feet the entire game.

The game itself was a defensive slugfest. We entered the 4th quarter down 9–3. I was sunburned, drunk, sipping whiskey we'd smuggled in, and screaming like a man possessed.

Then it happened.

On 4th and 12, Jason Campbell hit Courtney Taylor right in front of us for a first down. The place exploded.

A few plays later, 3rd and 12, Campbell hit Taylor again—this time in the corner of our end zone. Our end zone. It felt like an earthquake ripped through the stadium. 9–9. Tied.

We lined up for the go-ahead extra point.

Missed.

But then, a flag was thrown, penalty called. It was on LSU. We got another shot.

Vaughn lined up again.

Drilled it. 10–9.

Seconds left.

LSU tried one last time.

Interception—Junior Rosegreen.

Game over. Auburn beat the defending national champs. 3–0 start. None of us had a clue this season was going to become legendary.

I was there when we beat Tennessee in Knoxville—Ronnie Brown plowing through defenders as we embarrassed them 34–10. I stood in Jordan-Hare when we crushed Arkansas, Kentucky, and even Georgia.

And then it was time for the Iron Bowl.

Now, as I've mentioned, I grew up in a Bama family and Bama area. Auburn was a bad word. Back then, I hardly knew anyone who openly rooted for Auburn. This was going to be my first Iron Bowl live, and it was in Tuscaloosa.

They hated us for coming in undefeated and ranked #2.

They spit at us. Cussed at us. Flipped us off. Screamed in our faces. And early on, Alabama was winning. It stoked that fire of hate even more. But in the second half, Auburn surged back. We showed who the better team was. Pulled it out. Victory.

That night, we started celebrating with some folks we knew from back home who went to Bama. But even the strongest high school bonds couldn't survive the Alabama-Auburn line. Tensions were high. Real high.

So, we bounced, headed to meet up with more Auburn folks at a bar across town.

We were driving in an SUV with Auburn stickers, a flag flying from the window. Then came the blue lights.

We were doing 43 in a 55-mph zone. What was the reason?

"The vehicle swerved a little a few miles back."

All four of us had to get out, hands on the car, while they searched us. For what? Who knows. The driver hadn't had a drop, but us three? We were lit.

The cop said he didn't have a breathalyzer, so the driver had to go to the station for "further evaluation." The rest of us? We were driven to a random gas station on the edge of town and left there.

I swear to God, the cop smirked and drove off.

We had to use the gas station phone to call for help.

Our driver? He got to the station, blew clean, and was told to call someone to come get him.

I never went back to T-Town again.

But next fall? Oh, I remembered. But that's a story for another time.

That 2004 Auburn team... Hell, they didn't just ride momentum—they dragged it behind them like a ragin' bull that wouldn't quit. We made it to the SEC Championship that December, a rematch with Tennessee. Only this time, they weren't just rolling over. They came swinging, like they remembered every yard Ronnie Brown and Carnell "Cadillac" Williams snatched from them back in Knoxville. It was a fight. The kind of game where you grind your teeth for four quarters and leave the field blood-stained but grinning.

We pulled it off, though—38 to 28. Auburn was crowned SEC Champions.

We celebrated that night like the whole damn world spun in orange and blue. The bars on Magnolia were slammed full of bodies—shoulder to shoulder, drinks in the air, strangers turning into best friends and war brothers within seconds. Hell, we—Saxton, Daniel, me—weren't just watching history. We were living it.

But that whole season came with a dark cloud that no amount of whiskey or confetti could wash away. The USC Trojans—Matt Leinart and that firecracker Reggie Bush—were putting on a show out west. The media loved 'em. ESPN practically kissed their cleats every damn night. And because we got whooped by 'em back in 2003—different team, different time—they held that against us.

Even though we were undefeated in 2004.

Even though we beat four Top 10 teams.

Even though we played in the toughest conference in college football.

They gave the title shot to Oklahoma.

We got sent to the Sugar Bowl in New Orleans to face Virginia Tech, like it was some consolation prize wrapped in Mardi Gras beads and hushpuppies.

And we won that Sugar Bowl, 16–13. We scratched and clawed that W out in the Superdome, while USC steamrolled Oklahoma 55–19 like they were playing intramurals.

I sat on that couch back in Auburn, beer in hand, watching it all go down. Watching the media drool over that USC blowout. Knowing deep in my gut that Auburn would've given 'em hell. That it should've been us. Every player on that Auburn team knew it. Every student. Every damn barstool prophet in every dive from Opelika to Montgomery knew it.

But what can you do?

We partied like champions anyway. Because we were. We just didn't get the crown.

That night, the party bled into the streets. One keg turned into two, and by the time it was winding down, Saxton, Daniel, and I found ourselves walking out of a jam-packed apartment off Glenn, arms around each other, dragging a half-drained keg like it was a trophy.

Somebody—can't remember who—offered us the whole damn thing on our way out. Said, "Y'all take it—keep the night going." So, we loaded it into Dustin's truck, all of us howling like lunatics, and took off. Only problem? That street was one-way, and we went the wrong damn direction.

Of course, Auburn PD showed up. Right place, wrong time.

Blue lights lit us up like a firecracker, and Dustin got yanked from the vehicle. DUI. No negotiation. Didn't matter that we were blocks from home. Didn't matter that it was one of the most electric nights in Auburn history.

Cops let us off easy—made us unload the keg and walk it off into the night. Which we did. Laughing. Stumbling. Still undefeated. Still SEC champs. Still bitter. Still proud.

Auburn would finish 13–0 that year. USC would get to plant their flag. But everyone who knew ball—really knew it—knew Auburn was the real story.

And for me? That fall on the Plains?

It was the wildest ride of my life.

But the real wildness came just before the bowl games in January: Finals and the end of the fall semester.

Between hangovers, missed alarms, and half-read textbooks, I was hanging on by my fingernails. Every Sunday night I promised myself I'd straighten up, and by Thursday, I was right back in the madness.

Somehow, I passed.

I still don't know how I passed, but I did, and I made enough A's and C's, along with one D, to meet the required GPA.

In the back of my mind, I wondered just how long I could keep scraping by. It wasn't that I didn't care—it was that I didn't know how to slow down. After years of loss, anger, and running, I'd finally found something that felt good, and I was terrified of losing it.

43

BODDA GETTA AND GOODBYE

After that fall semester ended, I knew I'd have to make the pilgrimage back to Sand Mountain for Christmas—back to see Mama and Dad and the few family members that were still above the ground. Of course, I'd go back to visit Grandpa and Brittany's resting places again—just to sit, remember, and be still for a while. Couldn't imagine being that close and not stopping by.

I'd just gotten the news that I'd made it through the semester, my GPA still holding strong enough to not be ashamed. Look at me... Raye kid with six college semesters under his belt—one and a half of them from big Auburn University. I drove that trip back up Central East Alabama to the northeast corner of the state with something I hadn't carried in a while: pride. War Damn Eagle pride!

First stop on the mountain was the old gas station. The one that had sold me smokes when I was fifteen, back before I even knew what Marlboro meant besides a punchline in a country song. I'd fueled up there and fueled my lungs plenty since. I pulled up that day with my Auburn flag flying high off the car window, feeling like some prodigal hillbilly returning home with credentials.

But the old man who usually rocked on the porch and smoked his pipe while waving at everybody wasn't waving. Wasn't rocking. Just stared.

"Where you goin'?" he said flatly as I walked up.

I blinked. "Just grabbing some smokes and gas. How've you been?"

He raised a hand, palm out like a crossing guard, pulled the pipe from his mouth, and adjusted the elephant symbol on his crimson shirt, peeking out from beneath his overalls.

"We don't sell to your kind," he said.

I laughed. He didn't.

His son stepped out from behind the register, voice like a sidekick in a spaghetti Western.

"Yeah, boy," he said. "We don't sell to Auburn fans around here. Best head on down the road."

So, I turned, still chuckling, and shouted, "War Eagle!" as I slid into my car and rolled off.

By the time I hit the next curve, I was no longer laughing. My jaw was locked with my knuckles white on the steering wheel. It wasn't about football. It was about belonging. Suddenly, the place that once sold me my first pack of smokes was looking at me like I was some outsider who'd forgotten where I came from. Maybe they were right. Maybe I had.

The next station was corporate-owned. Sold to anybody with a pulse and a card. Still, the feeling of wrongness didn't quite leave me.

That Christmas break felt different. I hadn't been home in months, and already the house felt like it had rearranged itself in my absence. My room was now Dad's. Mama and he had started sleeping in separate rooms. Said they got better rest that way. My brother's room had been converted into a second bathroom.

Still, the walls told stories. Pictures from the past: the farm, school dances, Saxton, Ryan, elementary pool parties, prom photos with Brittany. Ghosts, all of it. Sweet, gut-punching ghosts.

We made the rounds, visited some family, exchanged laughs, and casseroles. But it was clear. This wasn't my place anymore. Never really had been. Too many ghosts. Too much meth. That plague had sunk deep claws into the mountain.

I stopped by a buddy's old house, just to check in. The place looked like a junkyard with memories of the past. His mom answered the door with a broken voice. Said he'd run off with a cousin in the middle of the night after trying to steal forty bucks from her purse. Meth again. Nobody had seen him in three months.

I checked on Brent, too. Turned out he'd moved to Huntsville. Did two years at the junior college and mourned the death of Blockbuster.

And then December 19th rolled around. I turned 21.

No bar crawl. No shots. No crawling back to a frat house floor.

I celebrated legally what I'd already lived illegally: drove home, ate at Kim San's Chinese place in the Valley, and messed around on my Sony Ericsson P900 cell phone. That was it. The break was over soon after.

Spring semester rolled in, and I had four business prereqs on the schedule: Intro to MIS, Operations Management, Principles of Management, and Consumer Behavior. I didn't know it yet, but I was about to become the co-founder of a tradition: the Welcome Back party.

Saxton and I threw the first one that spring. His trailer was the battleground. Four kegs, 25-50 people expected. That number more than tripled once the sun went down. Nearly got evicted from the trailer park.

Somehow, at some point, I climbed up on something— maybe a cooler, maybe a busted table—and gave a rockstar-style "thank y'all for coming" speech, closing out with a loud, slurred Bodda Getta chant.

My 20/20 persona had arrived in Auburn.

Spring brought new sports, and that's when we discovered Auburn softball. Holly Blur — an Eagle High School phenom in women's sports — had signed with AU and came in like a wrecking ball. She'd go on to break records, but back then, she was just our friend who sometimes showed up at parties.

One night, she damn near tackled one of our buddies through the underpinning of our trailer. The guy had been talking junk, insisting he "wouldn't hurt her." They lined up in a three-point stance to see who was stronger. We called it out — "Down... set... hut!" — and Holly launched him about five yards straight back, flat on his backside, nearly under the trailer. Then she just stood up, brushed off her hands, and walked away like it was nothing.

We'd get invited to some of the softball team's parties, too. Total game-changer. These girls didn't grow up on Sand Mountain. They were from New York, Miami, California, all over the place. We were like exotic zoo animals to them. They loved our accents, our wild stories, our downhome weirdness.

In return, we got to drink beer in living rooms filled with half-dressed collegiate athletes who had no romantic interest in us but appreciated us as mascots of a different culture. I wasn't complaining.

Classes kept getting tougher, but for the first time, I was genuinely interested in them. I started to grasp what business was really about. Not just breaking your back to impress a shift manager at some plant, but thinking, building, planning. It gave weight to what I'd told Blockbuster back in the day—that maybe I had more in me than I knew.

But something kept creeping in.

I had no idea what I was going to do if this all worked out.

If I got that degree... then what?

Where would I live? How would I work, feed myself, survive?

At that time, I was working afternoons at a fuel station out on Moores Mill Road—the "rich" side of Auburn. Professors lived out there. Athletic coaches. Old money and new tech wealth. Those were the sorts who moved around on that side.

Then there was me. Raye kid. Behind the register, making $9.50 an hour, ringing up protein bars and Marlboros for guys who drove Beamers and wore loafers with no socks.

I covered food, cigs, and booze. Dad helped with the trailer rent. Saxton covered the rest—for now. What funded the kegs and the bar tabs and the spontaneous trips to nowhere?

Government student loans. They came to you back then. Smiling. Shoveling money like candy. I'd learn the catch later. But at the time, I only took a fraction of what others did. That counted for something. Right?

As spring faded into early summer, I knew a decision was

coming.

Go home?

Or stay and work?

Saxton made it easy. He told me late in the semester that he wouldn't be coming back in the fall. Said he was chasing a music dream. I understood. His band had gotten good—grown into something with real legs.

That left me, Kelly, and her boyfriend Dustin in the trailer.

We threw a farewell party for Saxton, but deep down, I knew I'd need to find my own place soon. That chapter was closing, and a longtime friendship was changing yet again.

When Saxton left the next morning, the trailer felt hollow in a way I didn't expect. We'd been through fights, losses, and hangovers together; we'd grown together from bicycles to ATVS to cars, through relationships, breakups, parties, and deaths, but this was different. He wasn't just a friend—he'd been a witness to everything I'd survived. He was the brother that I wished really was. Watching him go felt like my continuous curse of losing someone.

It was another goodbye that stained me, left me reeling. But I did what Rayes do best: swallowed the ache and kept pushing along.

I passed my classes. Kept the bills covered.

Decided not to take summer classes, just work, save, and live in the quiet season of Auburn. With most students gone, it felt like a different town. Smaller. Still. Like I could breathe a little.

Fall would come again, like it always did.

And with it, whatever came next.

44
STORM PARTY

Saxton left, so I left. He had gone to chase chords and chords of dreams. Kelly stayed, but we were oil and water, and I'd had my fill. So, I moved. Pulled the trigger on a 1970s single-wide just short of collapse. Floor bowed in the kitchen like it'd taken a gut punch. Walls thin as a preacher's patience. Windows leaked even when it wasn't raining. Shower stall moaned underfoot like it was giving up the ghost. But it was mine. That counted.

Couldn't swing it alone, not with college bills and gas and smokes and late-night food. So, I brought in Cole Blade. Valley High, same age, same sense of humor. Cole had one hand like a folded map, just a thumb and a nub. Six fingers total. We made a pair, with me and my one good eye. We laughed about it more than most would.

Our lot sat right up front in Ridgewood Village, so we painted handicap symbols in our parking spots, told everyone we were Lot 12—handicapped by birth, not by choice. You had to laugh or you'd cry. That first morning, I pissed off the front porch, like I was still back home. Mid-stream, I hear the wheeze of air brakes. Tiger Transit, the college bus, stopped across the road. The whole damn bus full of students stared while I held myself in one hand and gripped the porch post with the other. Welcome to the neighborhood.

The fall semester was starting, and that meant a party. A big one. A "back to school" throwdown for the Sand Mountain crew and anyone who'd listen. Word spread. Friends old and new—Ryan was even transferring in. Seemed like every one of us misfit kids from red dirt and rock hollers was finding our way to Auburn. This was how we reunited.

That party? Bigger than we thought. Probably two hundred people at peak, spilling into the trailer, onto the porch, across the yard, and into the damn street. Cars choked the entry to the whole trailer park. You could smell weed, sweat, beer, the perfume of a girl dancing barefoot in my kitchen, and more. Music was shaking the paneling.

Then the storm came.

The wind blew sideways. Thunder like God's own bar fight. Rain didn't fall—it poured like judgment. And no one left. They all packed into that trailer, held together with duct tape and stubbornness. Inside, it was elbow to elbow, ass to cheek, sweat and smoke climbing the walls.

Mid-War Eagle chant, the lights cut. Power out. Pitch black, but no one missed a beat.

"WAAAARRR—

EEAAAAGGLLLE—

HEYYYYY!"

We roared it anyway. Storm or no storm. Power or no power. That party would not die. Cole and I collapsed sometime after 4 a.m., bodies scattered on couches, beer puddles pooling underfoot, ashtrays overflowing. The next morning, the smell hit first. Barroom stench, sharp and sour. Smoke, spilled liquor, bodies that hadn't showered in days. We cleaned for hours. Sprayed, scrubbed, swept, febreezed, opened every window. Still smelled like sin and cigarettes.

That party got us Strike One from the Ridgewood Village owners. We laughed it off. Wouldn't be the last.

Later that day, I pulled up Myspace. Had to reshuffle the Top 10 friends. Hurt feelings and drama always followed a good party. Who showed up, who didn't. Who flirted, who fought. That Top 10 was sacred territory back then—make one change and you were starting a war. Social landmines in digital form.

Somebody brought up that new site, too.

"You seen it? Facebook? Used to be 'The Facebook.' Like dropping the 'The' makes it cooler."

We laughed.

"Shit's never gonna beat Myspace."

Yeah, right.

But back then, we didn't know. We didn't know Facebook would take over, that Myspace would fade. That life would stop being measured in Top 10 friends and start being tracked in blue thumbs and news feeds. We didn't know anything, really.

Except this—we were broke, hungover, and grinning like fools in a busted-up single-wide trailer.

Yet somehow, we were happy.

45

RIVALRY IN BATON ROUGE

The fall of 2005 wasn't easy. I had two business classes, World Literature, and an easy elective I picked just to keep the GPA afloat. The elective didn't require much—just show up and participate, and I could pass. But the others? They were heavy. Every semester felt like I was balancing school, work, and keeping that state aid by the skin of my teeth.

The saving grace, once again, was Auburn football. Coming off that magical, undefeated season in '04, the expectations were still sky high, even though most of the badasses from that team were gone to the NFL. The season didn't start well. Georgia Tech came into Jordan-Hare and beat us. I was there. Watched it from the stands. It was like watching someone punch your best friend in the face, and you couldn't do a damn thing about it.

But we bounced back. Rattled off five wins behind Brandon Cox, Kenny Irons, and that hell-raising defense led by Travis Williams and Stanley McClover. Then came the LSU game. In Baton Rouge. At night. We'd all heard the stories about LSU's night games. Unholy. Wild. Pure, Cajun madness. Dustin, Ryan, and I decided to make the trip. A recent hurricane had made hotel planning tough, so we stayed the night before in Natchez, Mississippi, about two hours away.

That's where I met my first casino.

It was like Vegas light, draped in riverboat nostalgia. I'd played poker online and at home with buddies, but this was different. I walked in with wide eyes and a wallet barely holding together. We drank and wandered—eventually, we got separated. I had ten bucks left to my name, maybe five in my bank account.

I slid that last ten into a slot machine on my way out, fully ready to go cry in the car. And then—

Lights. Bells. Coins.

The machine screamed. People gathered. A server handed me a bucket. I didn't even check the total, just sprinted to the cashier. $325. Handed to me like a lifeline from God. I sat outside on the boat ramp and waited for the boys, holding my cash like it was a newborn.

The next morning, we woke up early and eager. We were two hours from LSU country, and we'd heard the tales. Rabid fans. Chaos. Corndogs.

That ride down, we were loud, proud, blasting tunes and chanting "War Damn Eagle" like we were marching into a friendly neighborhood.

We were not.

Reality hit at a red light near the stadium. The SUV rocked.

LSU fans—hundreds of them—surrounded us, pounding the windows, chanting, laughing. The air was thick, humid, smelled like beer and grease and goddamn corndogs. We sat frozen on a green light, not daring to move. They finally let us pass, laughing like they'd just poked the bear and dared it to growl.

We parked in a lot where some other Auburn fans were. Maybe 75 of us. But we were swallowed by thousands.

Kids—five years old maybe—ran up to us, flipped us off, and darted away like it was a game.

Dustin got hit in the back of the head with a beer can. The whole walk to the stadium felt like a gauntlet. No cops stopped them. No one stepped in. Pure hatred. And it was real.

Ryan and I had seats down low. The rest were seated in the upper deck. We stuck out like sore thumbs. Even the ushers gave us shit. We cheered, and they threatened to throw us out. Honestly, we felt the tension of the rabid fan base closing in on us, each play it felt like a tidal wave that was about to capsize at any second and swallow us whole.

The game itself? Brutal. Brilliant. Beautiful.

It was tied at the end. Went into overtime. And just like 2004... a missed field goal but this time no flag, no penalty, no retry—LSU won. 20-17.

Ryan and I got separated in the chaos. I walked alone, trying to meet them at a pre-planned spot. I tried to ignore the feeling of unease that hit me, hairs standing up. I was in enemy territory, and I was by myself. That was when I heard it—the LSU student section pouring out.

I was a speck of orange and blue in a sea of purple and gold.

They swarmed me.

Pushed. Spit. Someone knocked my Auburn hat off and stomped on it. I balled my fists, thought about swinging, but instead ducked my head and shielded myself. One against fifty wasn't worth it. The odds weren't in my favor, and I wasn't stupid enough to push my luck. The kid who power bombed Paul through the table and threw fists at games raged inside of me, but I wasn't that kid anymore.

I had grown at least enough to understand consequences, and this little mountain boy was out of his league, deep in unknown territory. So, even if everything in me was screaming at me to fight back, even if I knew a younger version of me would have tried to claw his way out, I chose to wait out the storm and let it pass.

Cops watched from across the street. Did nothing.

Eventually, I escaped the horde, them losing interest. I could still feel their suffocating presence, hear their screaming tones. Every step I took away from them should have brought relief, but it felt like my body was on fire.

When Ryan and Dustin found me, I was still quiet. Still burning.

We didn't stick around. Drove straight through the night in silence until we hit the Alabama line.

Back home, we didn't talk about the loss. We remembered the fight. The hate. For the first time, I understood what a real rivalry looked like.

And I never forgot it.

46

IRON BOWL REDEMPTION

That season, we went on to win three more games after the heartbreak in Baton Rouge, clawing our way toward the Iron Bowl, which was in Auburn this time. The memory of that LSU loss haunted me more than I expected. Not just the missed kick in overtime, not just the cruel twist of fate, but everything that surrounded it. The silence on the drive back to the Alabama state line. The feeling of being spit on and shoved by people who didn't know me but hated the colors I wore. The way no one stepped in. Not even the cops.

LSU fans were like wild animals that night—caged all week, let loose under the lights. But the thing that stuck with me most wasn't the loss. It was how I was made to feel as if I was less than human. Surrounded. Mocked. Alone in a sea of purple and gold with a torn hat and a busted ego.

I carried that with me back to Auburn. It festered. It fueled me.

When I looked at the calendar and saw the Iron Bowl on the horizon, I knew this one had to be different. This wasn't just about the game. It was about pride. About family. About

Auburn. We were riding a three-year win streak against Alabama, and this year, they were rolling in with Mike Shula and a top-10 ranking. The stakes were high, the tension higher. The whole week leading up to the game had an electricity that pulsed through the streets of Auburn. Classes started cancelling around Tuesday. Professors knew attendance was going to be laughable. By Wednesday morning, tailgating spots were staked, claimed, and fortified like war zones.

Back home, the mountain was practically empty. We had upwards of 50 people from Sand Mountain living or staying in Auburn by then. Some who were finishing their degrees, some who had moved down just to live the life, some just looking for a good time, and they all made the pilgrimage for this Iron Bowl.

So, I knew. We had to throw the party. The party that would define this rivalry weekend.

I teamed up with my buddy Tator, a Valley native, older than me, full of wit and charm. He had a good-sized trailer with a perfect yard and an even better setup inside. We moved furniture into rooms, cleaned the place up, and planned every detail like a military operation. The back bar was my post. We stocked it with every type of liquor you could think of, red solo cups stacked like a fortress, and music queued up for hours.

That Friday night before the game? It was unforgettable.

We expected maybe a couple of hundred. But word had gotten out, and before we knew it, Wire Road was lined with cars, people pouring in like a sea of orange, blue, crimson, and white. It was packed. Easily a thousand strong. Kegs floated one after another. Bottles emptied. The bass from the speakers rattled the trailer walls. Right in the thick of it all were

Alabama fans. They'd come with our friends from back home, and not once were they made to feel how we had been treated in Tuscaloosa the year before. Not once.

We served them shots. We welcomed them to the bar. We shouted and laughed and danced on the same damn beat. Because Auburn is different. We might wear different colors, but we don't treat you like garbage because of it.

That was the difference between us and them.

I remembered that moment outside the LSU stadium, my hat on the ground, my back against the wall, feeling like I was about to swing on a dozen drunk Cajuns. I looked around at our party—Alabama fans with Auburn fans, arms slung over each other's shoulders, singing along to Garth Brooks and Lil Jon, taking shots together like old war buddies. No violence, no hostility. Just a good time.

Because down here in Auburn, we might hate your team, but we don't hate you.

That night, I stood on top of Tator's trailer and looked out over a sea of people, music thumping, lights glowing, drinks flowing. I raised my glass and hollered the loudest damn "Bodda Getta" chant you've ever heard.

"Waaaaarrrrr Eagle!"

And the crowd answered, sounding like thunder rolling through the valley. The vibe was perfect for the rest of the night. Shots taken, bodies dancing, all equaling a good time had.

When we woke up the next morning, the house was wrecked. Solo cups in the sink. Strangers passed out on couches. Some girl—no idea who—had passed out in Tator's closet. Half-dressed, smeared makeup, confused, and asking for a name we didn't recognize. Her ride? Equally unknown.

Just another night in Auburn.

And then came gameday.

I stood inside Jordan-Hare Stadium, drunk on bourbon and adrenaline, watching our defense crush Brodie Croyle play after play. Eleven sacks. Eleven times we buried him in the grass. The crowd roared louder every time, like we were watching a ritual.

That was the difference.

Last year, I'd left T-Town upset at how they treated us. That year, I left Jordan-Hare a damn king.

And the memory of LSU? It still burned. But now I had something brighter to keep it company. Honk if you sacked Brodie!

But you know what else got sacked that semester?

My GPA.

47

THE NO CLASS CREW

Another fall had come and almost gone, and Christmas break was creeping closer. But this time it wasn't just the chill in the air that had me nervous—it was the realization that for the first time in my college career, I was staring down academic probation. My GPA had slipped. I was failing classes I shouldn't have failed. I'd declared my major too late and filled my earlier semesters with just enough elective fluff to party and keep that GPA floating. It was all catching up with me now.

Christmas came and went. I didn't go home that year. I had to work the day before and the day after the holiday. Mama and Dad drove down to Auburn to see me instead. The spring semester showed up fast, and with it, five business classes staring me down. Three of them were logistics-specific. It felt real suddenly—like the pretend game of college was now demanding answers.

By this time, football season had come and gone, and I wasn't following Auburn sports outside of the girls' softball team. Holly, our old friend from Eagle High, was breaking records, and we'd occasionally sip whiskey out of solo cups in the bleachers while cheering her on. Back then, Auburn basketball was barely a whisper compared to what Bruce Pearl turned it into years later. I once wandered into a basketball game by accident, just by following a rowdy crowd, and got handed free hot dogs, a soda, and a T-shirt. Pulled the pint of bourbon from my book bag and poured a little into the soda. Watched a half, then left. That's how disconnected I was.

Classes were rough, but I still had a way of finding my rhythm. Come home from work, and there might already be a party in full swing at Lot 12. All it took was a kiddie pool, five cases of Keystone Light, a bag of ice, and a little music, and suddenly a Tuesday looked like a Saturday.

Somewhere around that time, I got the bright idea to get over my fear of spiders. From watching the movie *Arachnophobia* as a kid, I'd carried that unease into adulthood. So, I bought a tarantula. Seemed like the right way to conquer it. That is, until one day, I came home from class, ready to feed the thing, and found it belly-up. Dead—or so I thought. Leaned in, lifted the lid, and out from the foliage came a bigger, meaner version. Turns out it had molted. I packed it up and carried it back to the pet store the very next morning.

Then someone—might've been Tator's girlfriend—asked me to babysit her pet boa constrictor. So, suddenly, our busted-ass trailer had both a tarantula and a snake. One night, the boa escaped and slithered to the top of our fridge, knocking things over. When I saw it up there, tongue-flicking and peering down, I knew I was in over my head. I returned that creature not long after, too. But the real flavor that spring came from the crew I was hanging with. New friends with names like Big

Will, Bryan and Cam (the brothers), Jamie, and this wiry little hellraiser we called Whiskey. Most of them were from Georgia or small-town Alabama. None of them were students. They just came to Auburn during its golden age to get local jobs and party on the side.

Big Will was a walking myth. Seven foot something, four hundred pounds, and the kind of guy that could silence a room with just a look. One night at Supper Club, some guy was talking trash at me—I can't even remember why. Probably flirted with his girl, who knows. He came up chest puffed, ready to swing, and I puffed back, thinking I was some kind of mountain-bred badass. Dude suddenly backed down. Started stammering and mumbling excuses. I felt ten feet tall... until I turned around and there stood Big Will, arms crossed, staring a hole through the guy's soul. That was when I knew my little beer belly ass didn't do shit. Will was the real enforcer. When he was around, we were untouchable.

Big Will wasn't the only one who gave our little circus its flavor. Bryan and Cam—the brothers—were the kind of guys who could turn a trip to Walmart into a full-blown adventure, and boy, could they punish some cold ones. Jamie always had a new scheme or side hustle, and even though he was the oldest of this group, he was the right amount of crazy it needed, and Whiskey... well, Whiskey was a six-foot fuse with no off switch on alcohol and fun. We weren't students anymore, not really. We were just a crew of drifters orbiting Auburn's gravity, holding on to youth a little longer than we should have. This group was epic in ways that the previous ones couldn't master as we were not kids, but we damn sure were fighting like hell not to be full-blown adults yet either. We partied like it was our job. Days at the pool, nights under porch lights. Even when storms rolled in, someone had a roof and some cold beer. It was all laughs and stories. We didn't talk about futures or careers. We lived in the now. We were poor but happy.

For all our chaos, I loved those guys. They weren't my past—they were my pause. The world felt smaller with them, easier, like the clock had stopped for a while and nobody cared if we were winning or losing. They were exactly who I needed as the future loomed closer.

That spring, I watched as friends I had come down with graduated, degrees in hand, ready to move on. Others? They washed out, went home with nothing but debt and a hangover. And me? Somehow, I was still there. Hanging on with a 2.0 GPA—just enough to keep my place in the College of Business and my tuition paid.

I decided to take one summer class to keep myself grounded but spend the rest of the time soaking up Auburn. That turned out to be a terrible plan.

We called ourselves the "no class crew" that summer. Pool parties every day. Beer by the case. Whiskey on demand. Our skin went bronze, our livers went to war, and we probably pissed in pools more than we flushed toilets. It was glorious and a little pathetic.

The class I took that summer met on Tuesdays and Thursdays at 11 a.m. I'd show up in swim trunks, tank top, sunglasses, smelling like chlorine and last night's regrets. One day, I brought a small shoulder cooler to class. Half drunk, half hungover, I cracked open a Natty Light mid-lecture. The professor looked up, stunned.

"Mr. Raye," he said, "I've been teaching here for sixteen

years. I don't know if I'm impressed or deeply concerned."

He didn't kick me out. Just told me to get my act together. I wore khakis and a polo to every class after that and walked out with a B. Should've been an A, but hell, I deserved the B just for not getting expelled.

As the summer faded, I sat down one night, looked in the mirror, and asked myself: *What now?* I had no damn idea. But I knew football season was coming again—and that was reason enough to keep showing up.

48
ACADEMIC SUSPENSION

The fall semester rolled in, and I was nowhere near ready to take it seriously. The classes were harder, the material was heavier, and it started to interfere with the one thing I had mastered: being the life of the party. Reality was creeping in like a slow fog over Sand Mountain, and I started wondering if maybe everyone back home was right. Maybe I was in over my head. Sure, I'd graduated high school, and I had what—six semesters of college under my belt? But without a piece of paper to prove it, it didn't mean much.

So, I thought if this thing was going to fall apart, I might as well ride it 'til it did. Because soon enough, I'd have to face the real world, and that little gas station job over on Moores Mill wasn't gonna cut it. Twenty hours a week at $9.50 an hour wasn't going to feed me, house me, and keep me in cold Keystone.

I had dated here and there over the past few semesters, caught feelings a couple of times, but nothing really stuck. Honestly, the real relationship was between me and Auburn— the nightlife, the football, the backyard parties, and trailer park chaos. By then, most of my closest friends weren't even in school. They had jobs around town or were just floating through the college scene like I was, trying to hold onto the glory days for as long as they could.

Football season was the one thing still holding everything together. Our tailgate spot had become legend—home base for Northeast Alabama. We were down in the heart of Auburn, but every weekend, it felt like a Sand Mountain reunion. We'd hold our ground with coolers and grills and war damn eagle chants that echoed across campus.

The team was solid again that year. We finished 11-2, beat Alabama in the Iron Bowl (again). While I refused to go back to Tuscaloosa, I heckled enough LSU fans at our home game to make up for it. That one was a war—top ten matchup, low-scoring slugfest. We edged them out 7-3. It felt good.

But behind the fun, my grades were tanking. Right before Christmas break, I got the call. My academic advisor wanted a meeting. Now, when they request a meeting, it's never good.

I sat in her office with that pit-in-your-stomach feeling, like being called to the principal's office.

My advisor looked over her glasses and said it plainly, "Claxton, you're on academic suspension for one semester."

I blinked. "Okay... so, what electives can I take in the spring to bring my GPA up?"

She sighed and shook her head. "No, Claxton. You can't take anything. You're *suspended*. You have to sit out a semester."

It hit me like a brick. I asked about my tuition and the aid I was getting. My advisor said she'd have to report it. That was that.I walked out of her office hollow, thinking about every hallway I'd walked, every professor who'd believed in me, and every friend I'd made who might've already graduated or flunked out. I wandered through the business building until I found one of my favorite professors—one of the few who ever treated me like I had a real shot.

He waved me in.

"What do you need?" he asked without looking up from his desk.

"I need a miracle," I said.

Still writing, he said, "A lot of students do."

He asked if I planned on being a professional one day. I nodded.

"Where will you work? What city? What part of logistics? What job title are you aiming for?"

I stumbled over every word.

"That's why you're in my office right now," he said. Then he asked, "You know how many classes you have left to get your degree?"

I had no clue.

"Four," he said. "Just four."

Tears welled up. I felt like a complete failure.

Then he slid a piece of paper across the desk. "An internship just came in. Starts in January. It's paid. Newnan, Georgia. Nobody else has taken it. Sign this, figure out how to get there, and go work."

I signed it.

He said they'd tell the financial aid department that this internship was necessary for my professional development. It was their way of keeping me in the game.

I walked out with a flicker of hope.

A few days later, I was driving up I-59, heading home for

Christmas. First time back to Sand Mountain in probably 15 months. I had the windows down, the Auburn flag waving, blasting music. Every now and then, I'd pass a car flying an Alabama flag and throw up a five with my hand—five in a row, baby. Auburn fans gave it back with pride. Bama fans flipped me off like clockwork.

When I got home, it felt different. I was different.

I was one of the few who had made it out, and I was clawing to stay gone. I ran into some family, including the ones who'd stopped speaking to me after I became an Auburn man. They tried to talk about "the Bear" and the good ol' days. I just laughed and smiled. I'd earned that.

But even with all the wins and parties and memories, I knew I had almost lost it all.

It wasn't just school I was about to lose; it was Auburn itself. The late nights, the roar of Jordan-Hare, the feeling that I'd made it out of Sand Mountain and was finally building something of my own. For the first time in my life, I'd found a place that felt like mine, and I'd almost thrown it away chasing the idea that I had time to figure it all out.

I had four classes left. One more mess-up, and I wouldn't be able to finish what I started.

So, I was headed to a town I'd never heard of, Newnan, Georgia, for a job I didn't know anything about.

It wasn't Auburn. But it might just be the second chance I didn't know I needed.

Still, the drive toward Newnan felt different. I wasn't sure if I was being rescued or tested. Hope had a way of feeling a lot like fear back then, but either way, I just knew I wasn't finished yet.

49

THE LONG DRIVE TO NEWNAN

Newnan, Georgia.

It's about a 45 to 50-minute haul up I-85 from Auburn, on paper. That doesn't count the early mornings, the Eastern Time zone difference, or the traffic that started piling up as you neared Atlanta's outer rings. My alarm clock went off at 4:30 a.m. most mornings. By 5:00 a.m., I was on the road with a thermos of gas station coffee and a mind full of second thoughts. I'd traded in my student life of late-night tailgates and impromptu beer pong tournaments for this—a gray sky, a stretch of asphalt, and a car stereo humming out country songs and old rap hits while my headlights carved the dark.

Some mornings, I'd pass the same cars filled with people commuting to jobs they probably didn't love, just like I was trying to avoid. Other mornings, I'd see the parking lot of Fat Daddy's still lit up, still packed with the leftover wild ones from the night before, music still thumping behind their walls as I drove past, headed for the real world. I remember shaking my head, part jealousy, part pride. I used to be them. Now, I had a different kind of hangover: responsibility.

Those drives became my thinking time. Somewhere between mile marker 12 and the state line, I'd replay every turn that led me there—Brittany, the fights, the wasted nights, the way Auburn felt so close but out of reach. Some mornings, I wondered if I'd traded one kind of exhaustion for another. Other mornings, I told myself this was the price of growing up, the miles between who I was and who I wanted to be. I was determined to make something of the opportunity.

I was assigned to an internship at a 3PL (third-party logistics provider) inside the Yamaha plant in Newnan. I came in expecting grunt work—sweat and forklifts. But that was not what they had in mind. They didn't want my back; they wanted my brain. For the first time in my life, I was expected to *think* for a paycheck.

And let me tell you. I wasn't ready.

Not ready for meetings with executives who wore nice watches and spoke in bullet points. Not ready for discussions about routing algorithms and warehouse optimization. Not ready to be asked what I thought, not just what I could carry or clean. I was suddenly helping design manpower models, calculating cost-per-mile on shipping routes, and identifying bottlenecks in production schedules. I didn't know half the terms they used. I spent my first few weeks Googling acronyms under the table and scribbling down buzzwords like they were spells I had to learn to cast.

And yet... I liked it.

Maybe not at first, but the challenge was different than anything I'd faced before. This wasn't basketball practice, it wasn't the SAT, and it sure as hell wasn't trying to finish a six-pack before curfew. This was real. And I was doing it.

I'd get home wiped out. Not from physical labor, but from the mental gymnastics of the day. I'd flop onto the couch, dead tired, and Cole would ask how it went.

"Man," I'd say, "I think I used up every brain cell I had today."

What I didn't realize in those moments was that I was growing up. Slowly. Unevenly. Like a weed pushing through concrete.

As the weeks passed, something else crept up on me. I began to think about school again. I started looking back at how close I actually was to finishing that degree. And when I finally sat down and counted, it hit me. I had four classes left. *Four.* Four damn classes.

But it wasn't that simple. Two of those were back-to-back prerequisites: Business Calculus I and II. The very same classes I'd kicked down the road semester after semester, like a can I didn't want to deal with. Now, they were the gatekeepers to my future.

I knew I had to sign up for summer classes and take one—just one—to chip away at the wall. I decided to enroll in Business Calculus I that summer. But in doing so, I made a choice to stay in Auburn and study, instead of heading home or finding some easy way out.

Meanwhile, my presence at the local watering holes started to fade a little. I still made time for the weekend scene, sure. But more often than not, I'd trade a night of shots and smoky bars for a few hours of quiet, a Netflix DVD, or a long drive to clear my head.

Then May hit, and with it came an unexpected offer.

The company I'd been interning for, who had recently lost

a key employee, asked if I wanted to stay. Full-time. With a salary. They offered me the same job I'd already been doing, just with a real paycheck and a title.

The VP even sat me down and said, "You've proven yourself, Claxton. You know how to learn, and you know how to work. You could stay, you know. You could make a career out of this."

It was flattering. Terrifying. Tempting.

I asked about finishing my degree. He told me the company had tuition reimbursement after one year on the job. I could finish online. Lots of people did it.

I thought about it. *Hard.*

I imagined it. The steady income, a clean shirt every morning, maybe even my own place that didn't creak when you breathed. It was tempting as hell. The kind of stability nobody back home would ever talk you out of. But deep down, I felt that same old tug, the one that always showed up right before I sold myself short.

For a long night, I sat on the edge of my trailer bed and weighed it all. The parties. The years. The family pride. The silent sacrifices my parents made to get me to this point.

Then I thought about my professor. The one who told me I had four classes left. The one who pulled me out of the wreckage of academic suspension and gave me this shot.

I wasn't ready to settle. Not yet. I had fought so hard to get to college, and I felt that I would be quitting and losing something else again. So, I decided to finish what I started.

I turned down the job.

I signed up for summer classes.

I enrolled in Business Calculus I, the beast I had avoided for years.

In that moment, under the dull ceiling light of my ragged little trailer kitchen, surrounded by empty Keystone cans and the stale smell of sweat and ambition, I made a decision.

I was going to finish this damn thing.

No matter what it took.

50
SUMMER STRUGGLES

The sun never quite stopped bleeding heat over Auburn in the summer. That red dust haze shimmered off the blacktop like it was daring you to walk across it barefoot. The summer of 2007 came in like a heatstroke. I walked straight into it with four classes on my plate and every ounce of exhaustion still left in my bones from years of trying to become something I still wasn't sure I was meant to be.

Two of those classes were five-week burners. Blink and you missed it. Miss one day, and you're guaranteed a B or less. No excuses. No grace. That's the thing about summer classes. They were ruthless, fast, and they didn't care about your party schedule, your hangovers, or the heat that made your skin blister just standing still.

By the time I made the decision to finish this damn thing once and for all, I was already behind the game. Late registration meant scraping the bottom of the barrel for class options and professors. And if you were a student back then, you remember RateMyProfessor.com. It was the Bible of survival at Auburn. You avoided any teacher with more than three chili peppers in math or science unless you had a death wish. Four or five peppers? You'd better be a prodigy.

The only available Business Calculus I class had a four-pepper professor with a last name I couldn't pronounce and a reputation for grading like he was training you to solve quantum physics problems on Mars. The class was M-W at 10 a.m. Sharp. Relentless. Unforgiving.

I threw everything I had at it. All the old notebooks. Every bit of effort that I hadn't wasted on shot glasses and Keystone Light. It was my first math class since junior college, and I was staring at equations like they were written in Greek, and maybe some of them were.

I took the Tiger Transit more often than I'd like to admit. It saved the hassle of finding a decent parking spot. Even when I had the coveted A-zone pass, those spots vanished like gold during a rush. Sometimes, I'd sell that A-zone pass by the week. Pocketed good money off it. Made more than a gas station shift just for having it. But that particular morning, I stood in front of my busted single-wide, bag slung, mind buzzing, ready for class, waiting on the bus.

The bus came. I climbed in. Zoned out as it picked up more and more students. We were ten miles in when it stopped. Dead halt. Somewhere out on a strip of nowhere between trailer parks and hope. The driver radioed in. No ETA. No plan. I looked at my phone. 40 minutes to class. Two buses passed. Didn't stop. I made a decision.

I started walking.

Auburn summer. Thick air. Two hills. 8-year smoker. Beer belly and sweat pouring like someone left the faucet running inside me. By the time I hit the tennis courts across from where we used to tailgate, I was dying. Not metaphorically. Dying.

Made it to class. Ten minutes late. The professor didn't even blink.

"Absent," he said.

I argued. Pleaded. Told him to call the bus station.

He didn't. Said something I'll never forget.

"You're here because you made poor choices in the fall and spring. This is the consequence. In the real world, if you're late, you're late. Doesn't matter why. Just be on time next class."

I showed up thirty minutes early every day after that.

I dropped the Math class before it could hurt my GPA. That four-pepper bastard taught math like we were decoding time travel. I looked at him one day and felt hate—pure, tired, hopeless hate—and turned it inward.

I had to drop the class. Sat across from my counselor and watched the dream flicker again.

Dropping that class cost me more than time. It pushed graduation back another semester, threw my financial aid into question, and increased the feeling that I was not smart enough to beat math. It felt like every step forward came with two steps back, but I refused to back down. I had committed to finishing what I started.

So, it would have to be Spring '08. Another semester. Another round.

The end of summer came. The report card said I was back in good standing. I mapped the plan: two classes in the fall, two in the spring, and then, finally, graduation. But life was picking up. It wasn't just school anymore.

I met someone. She stuck around longer than most. She wasn't a passing fancy but someone I wanted to get to know.

Finally, life had reached a decent rhythm.

But then came the phone call.

The agency that paid my tuition—the one that saw my bad eye as reason enough to invest in me—had new leadership. The guy who'd believed in me? Gone. Replaced.

The new guy said I wasn't "disabled enough."

Just like that, the rug started slipping. Suddenly, I remembered. This was always borrowed time. And time, no matter how hard you fight it, always comes calling.

51

FINAL PUSH

I had a plan in place. It wasn't a good one, but it was mine. I could use student loans if needed to pay for that final class load, but I wasn't done fighting. Not yet. Not after everything. That new guy, the one who replaced the counselor who'd helped me get my tuition covered for years, came in swinging like he knew me. Like I was just another case number. He tried to pull the rug out, saying I wasn't "disabled enough." Hell, that was the same argument I had made years earlier, but suddenly it was being used to take away the very lifeline that got me to the 10-yard line.

It took an act of Congress—well, an act of a father with some pull and a few well-placed phone calls to the right folks—but I got reinstated. The deal was four classes across two semesters. No wiggle. No safety net. Finish school or come home and find work. Work that didn't come with a cap and gown. That fall, I was enrolled in Business Finance and Business Cal 1. One on Tuesday/Thursday at 9 a.m. and the other on Monday/Wednesday/Friday at 10 a.m. I also landed another paid internship, this time with CoachComm in Auburn. Shipping and receiving. Not the high-level logistics work like in Newnan, but it paid.

Funny thing was, if Coach Spurrier chucked a headset in a Saturday game, you could bet your ass it was sitting in my hands by Monday, scuffed and dented, ready to be repaired and shipped back by Thursday.

That girl from the summer? She moved into Lot 12. It was me, her, and Cole then, splitting bills and making life work. We were never some big love story. We met drunk. I think the first thing she said to me was, "Who are you talking to?" when I tried starting a conversation at the pool. She didn't realize I was looking at her with my good eye as the left one had a mind of its own. I laughed, she laughed, and we just kind of stuck. Not love. Not really. More like keeping each other company in a town that was slowly starting to shift beneath our feet.

Fall football came around, and I had a new mission: Get my dad to a game. He'd never been inside a college stadium before, and I figured it was time. I bought us tickets, far from the chaos of the student section. We sat in the endzone opposite the Auburn students. Auburn vs. South Florida, a night game, and the air was electric. For a few hours, my dad wasn't a tired man with decades of work in his bones. He was waving an orange and blue shaker and soaking it all in. We lost that night. Go-ahead touchdown scored right in front of us. That stadium emptied out like someone pulled a plug in a bathtub. But I didn't care. My dad had finally seen it.

By mid-semester, I was holding my ground in both classes. I even hired a tutor for the math. CoachComm was manageable. Life was surprisingly steady. I scraped by Business Cal 1 with a D, that beautiful letter that meant diploma. That spring, I had just two classes left. It was strange, knowing that this thing I'd dragged behind me for so long was finally about to end.

Auburn itself was changing. No more trailers. The trailer parks were closing or being bought up for new condos and developments. Auburn was getting shinier, more expensive, and a little less rough around the edges. My friend Whiskey said it best: "The dinosaurs are dying off."

Spring 2008 came, and I could see the finish line. Every week that passed felt like the end of a chapter. My friends were gone. Married. Having kids. Working jobs in Huntsville, TVA, chicken farms, and law firms. Me? I was about to get my degree in Logistics, and the job market was dogshit. The recession had hit. The economy tanked. Interview calls were rare and mostly weird.

I flew to Dallas for one. First time flying. They picked me up in some stretch limo truck and scared the life out of me on those freeways. The interview was a dinner and then some rapid-fire panel Q&A the next day. I bombed. Hard. The whole time, I felt like a high school kid trying to bluff his way into the big leagues.

The next one was in Sioux Falls, South Dakota. Had to land in Omaha and drive two hours north. Beautiful, flat land. No clouds. They cut the trip short because of a snowstorm warning. I laughed—the sun was out, blue skies—and I had no idea why they were so cautious. But forty-five minutes later, I was in a blizzard. Whiteout. Screaming at the road, praying, calling home. Snowplows just passing by like freight trains. Somehow, I made it back to the airport. Watched them de-ice the plane three times before takeoff. Landed in Atlanta, kissed the ground, and knew South Dakota wasn't my future.

I tried reconnecting with the folks from Newnan. Gone. One moved to Michigan. CoachComm had no openings. Panic started to sink in. I had just asked that girl I lived with to marry me—felt like the right thing to do at the time. We planned a small wedding in Opelika.

May came. I met with my advisor. She smiled. I had Cs in both classes. Cs meant walking. I remember that feeling. Like a kid again. I had done it. Against all odds. I had gone from Eagle High standard track to a damn college graduate. My parents and one of my aunts came to see it. I walked across that stage and held my degree in Logistics.

I was one of the last to do so. Auburn changed the program to Supply Chain Management that year.

But the next day? Reality.

I'd crossed the stage, sure, but real life didn't hand out diplomas. It kept its tests coming.

52
SOUTHERN GOSPEL

By now, you're probably wondering what in the hell could possibly come next. I mean, really. How much more chaos could the Raye blood conjure up? You've read the fights, the failures, the parties, the heartbreaks, the comebacks. I graduated. Got the damn degree. I walked that stage with a C in Business Calc and a smirk only earned through six years of soul-wrenching, whiskey-soaked, sweat-stained grit. So, that's it, right?

Not even close.

If you've made it this far, you already know this wasn't just some feel-good redemption tale. This was my Southern gospel, verse by verse, from that one-eyed, crooked-smile little kid on Sand Mountain who had no business dreaming outside his ZIP code, to a college graduate walking across a stage in Auburn Arena, diploma in hand, heart still bruised, lungs full of fire. That wasn't a ceremony. That was a resurrection.

But if you think for one second that the luck of a Raye turns golden just because a diploma gets slapped into his palm, then you haven't learned a damn thing from this book. The story doesn't end here. It just pauses long enough to catch its breath. Just long enough to set the hook.

After Auburn, life hit hard. Like a freight train with no horn. The ink on my diploma wasn't even dry before the next chapter came roaring in. Soul-sucking jobs that promised futures but delivered ulcers. Marriage that burned like dry timber in the wrong season, leaving two beautiful kids in the ashes. The heartbreaks got deeper. The smiles came harder. And the mirror didn't lie. I'd aged. I'd hardened. I'd cracked. But I kept going.

There were stretches of years when I didn't know who the hell I was. Suit and tie in boardrooms, bar tabs in nameless towns, long nights staring out of windows with nothing but headlights on a wet road for company. The Raye blood doesn't go quietly. It simmers, then boils. And sometimes, it breaks.

But now? I'm in my 40s. Seasoned. Worn. But not beaten. Married to a beautiful woman who knows every scar I carry, some I didn't even have to explain. Her love would save me. Five amazing kids now. That's a whole basketball team and a sixth man, if you count the old me still pacing the sideline, yelling at referees called "life" who never blow the whistle fair.

And those kids? They don't even know yet what kind of gospel they're inheriting, but I have the experience to help them.

See, this book you just finished? It was just the first verse. A southern hymn of survival and foolishness, grit and grace, bad luck and bourbon-soaked blessings. It was backwoods redemption with a one-eyed lens and a whole lotta scars. It was trailer park theology. Dirt-road doctrine. It was a young man trying to outrun the ghosts of his last name with nothing but a rusted-out car, a fake ID, and a stubborn belief that maybe, just maybe, he could rewrite the ending.

But the next twenty years? Lord, help us all. Because if you thought the parties were wild, if you thought the fights were brutal, if you thought the heartbreaks were deep and the wins hard-earned—just wait. That Southern gospel keeps writing itself. In ink and fire and every damn lesson I never wanted but couldn't do without.

So, yeah. The road doesn't end here. I'll be back with the rest of the story.

And I promise.

You ain't ready.

ACKNOWLEDGEMENTS

This book exists because of the people who stood beside me long before I believed I had a story worth telling.

To my wife and children—thank you for your patience, your sacrifices, and your steady love while I chased words late at night. You are my reason and my grounding.

To my parents, family, and friends—thank you for shaping me, challenging me, and reminding me where I come from.

And to everyone who encouraged me to finally put these stories on paper—this book carries a piece of you as well.

ABOUT THE AUTHOR

Darin Brown is a Southern writer whose work draws from a childhood shaped by rural life, unspoken expectations, and the struggle to belong. In The Gospel According to a Southern Nobody, he reflects on growing up on Sand Mountain, Alabama, exploring how family, culture, poverty, violence, humor, and resilience formed him—sometimes by breaking him first. His writing is raw, reflective, and deeply rooted in lived experience. This is his first published book.

EMAIL   darin.brown1219@gmail.com

FACEBOOK   facebook.com/DarinBrown-Author

INSTAGRAM   @Darin.Brown1219